Aboke Girls
Children abducted in northern Uganda

Els De Temmerman

Fountain Publishers

Published as *De Meisjes van Aboke: Kindsoldaten in Noord-Oeganda*
by De Kern, Baarn, The Netherlands

Fountain Publishers Ltd
P.O. Box 488
Kampala, Uganda
(256) (41) 259-163 (tel), 251-160 (fax)
fountain@starcom.co.ug (e-mail)

ISBN 9970-02-256-3

Photographs: Courtesy of the author

Preface

It was rather accidently that I came across the story of the abducted children in northern Uganda when, in December 1998, I met Norman in the garden of a development worker in Gulu. The boy behaved strangely. He took up to ten showers a day, could not concentrate at school and was too scared to go home for Christmas. Sitting next to him in the garden, I listened to his story for hours. It was told in an emotionless, almost trivial way. It seemed too shocking to be true.

At the World Vision reception centre in Gulu, Norman's story was confirmed by other children who had escaped from the Lord's Resistance Army. The evidence was overwhelming. The escapees showed all the physical and emotional scars of the atrocities they described. Their stories were accurate, detailed and confirmed by other children, interviewed separately, at different places in northern Uganda.

I went back to northern Uganda seven times in the following two years and conducted in-depth interviews with the main characters in the book. Those particular children were picked out not because theirs were the most dramatic stories, but simply because their English was fairly fluent, because they were good at remembering details and were willing and able to talk about their experiences.

Everything in this book was checked with a second and often a third source. Ellen's story was verified with Grace's and Caroline's, two Aboke girls who also escaped in the first six months of their abduction. Sarah's testimony was checked with Justine, who was rescued from Sudan at about the same time as her. The five girls were then confronted with each other in order to sort out any differences or contradictions.

Norman's story was confirmed by his friend, Stephen, and by Yeko, a boy abducted in 1996 from Sir Samuel Baker School, who was repatriated from Sudan in April 2000. Sister Rachele's story was confirmed by John Bosco, the teacher who took part in the pursuit of the rebels, and by the Germany MP, Rudolf Decker, who was part of

i

the delegation to Sudan in April 1997. I met Mr Decker in Strasbourg and he was kind enough to let me use his diary of the journey to Sudan, which proved to be a valuable source of information.

The details of the meeting of the presidents in Eldoret were confirmed by the then Ugandan Minister of Defence. The visit of the Sudanese MPs to northern Uganda was related to me by three witnesses: Sister Rachele, George Omona and Keith Wright of Unicef. Other events, such as Sister Rachele's visit to the Gulu barracks, were backed up by video-footage or by newspaper articles. In the end , the manuscript was read and approved by all the characters.

With the exception of the camps of the Lord's Resistance Army, all the places described in the book were visited by me personally during my assignment as Africa correspondent for the Dutch newspaper *De Volkskrant* and Belgian Radio and Television, between 1992 and 1996.

The obstacles to writing this book were huge. First of all, there was the problem of communication. There were only a handful of telephone lines in northern Uganda, none of them accessible to any of the people in the book. A mobile phone network was only installed in Gulu in the middle of the year 2000. Obtaining additional information, or getting the manuscript to the different characters, was a difficult and time-consuming process.

Secondly, there was the problem of security. Although 1999 was a relatively quiet year, the rebels invaded the country again in December 1999, making the trip to the north more difficult and creating a security problem for the characters in the book. Children who escaped from the Lord's Resistance Army are still not safe. The risk of them being abducted again and killed, or punished for telling their story, is real. In order to protect them, their names have been changed in the book. By the time of publication of the English version of the book, all the children involved will have left the war area in northern Uganda.

I am deeply indebted to my characters, in the first place to Sister Rachele, for whom recalling the past was often a torment. I deeply admire her courage, persistence and her unconditional altruism. I thank Ellen, Sarah and Norman for sharing their painful stories with me. I was struck by their honesty, their courage and their ability to remain human in inhuman circumstances. Many thanks to Yeko, who scrupulously went through the manuscript, helped me with the chronology of events and provided me with precious details of the Lord's Resistance Army and its leader Joseph Kony.

My appreciation and gratitude also go to George Omona, Angelina Atyam and Rudolf Decker. Each in their own way, they fought and keep on fighting against this grave abuse of children. Decker gave me some insight in the discreet world of international diplomacy. Angelina let me feel what it must be like to be the mother of an abducted child. And George gave me an honest and objective understanding of the background of the conflict in northern Uganda.

I am obliged to the people of Gusco, World Vision, AVSI and Unicef for their kind cooperation and their assistance in interviewing the escapees. In particular, I wish to thank Hervé Cheuzeville of AVSI, without whom I would never have set foot in northern Uganda, and Jef Duyck in Kampala, whose tireless efforts to rent cars, offer accommodation and send manuscripts to the north have been of crucial importance. Without their help, the publication of this book would not have been possible. Last but not least I want to thank Mr and Mrs De Pauw for their kind help in correcting the English manuscript.

Els De Temmerman
January 2001

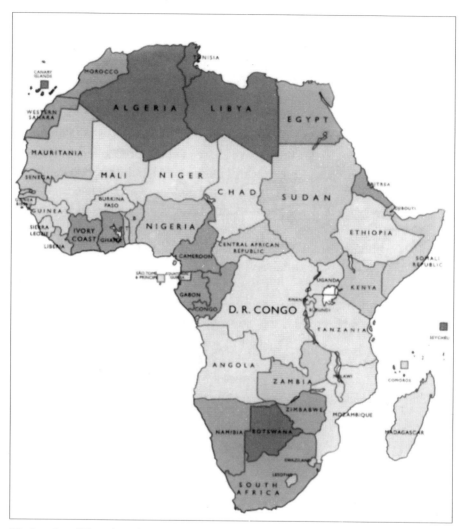

The location of Uganda and its neighbours in Africa

Most of the children abducted by the Lord's Resistance Army have been from Gulu, Kitgum, Lira and Apac districts in northern Uganda

Introduction: A spiral of violence

Uganda has finally shed its international reputation as a country of mass killings and gross human rights violations. With Idi Amin's reign of terror firmly consigned to the past, the country is now trying hard to regain its image as 'Pearl of Africa'. Since President Yoweri Museveni came to power in 1986, there has been increasing political stability and economic development. In the 1990s, Uganda had one of the fastest growing economies in the world, with an average annual growth rate of 7 percent between 1990 and 1997 (The Economist). Uganda is the first country in Africa to introduce universal primary education and to successfully reduce the spread of the AIDS epidemic.

But the northern part of the country has been largely excluded from this success story. In this area, roughly the size of Belgium, inhabited by about one million people, a forgotten war is going on, which has already claimed an estimated 100,000 lives.

The roots of the conflict go back to the period of colonial rule: the British administration recruited most of its civil servants from the south and most of its soldiers from the north. The people of the northern region (the Acholi and Langi) were made into the country's military elite. During the Second World War, their soldiers fought on the side of the British all over the world. But it was the fertile south, in particular the Buganda region, that enjoyed development and produced most of the country's intellectuals.

At independence in 1962, a delicate power balance was struck between the king of Buganda, who became the country's first president, and Prime Minister Milton Obote, a Lango from the north. It did not take long, however, for Obote to monopolise the power. In 1966, he ordered his Army Chief of Staff, Idi Amin, to storm the royal palace. The king was deposed and thousands of his followers were either loaded onto trucks and dumped in the River Nile at Murchison Falls or buried alive. From then on, violence became part of the political system: the key for settling political disputes.

In 1971, Obote himself was overthrown by his army commander, Idi Amin. Coming from the West-Nile region, Amin feared the influence of the Acholi and Langi in the army. He ordered the execution of hundreds of officers and replaced them with men of his own ethnic group. His notorious death squads then set about eliminating any opposition. Hundreds of thousands of people, including many northeners, were killed during Amin's eight years of rule. Many were beaten to death with hammers and iron bars or tortured in prisons and police stations all over the country. The economy collapsed, particularly after Amin expelled the large Asian population and nationalised the British plantations and companies. The general and his accomplices carried off the prize, valued at one-and-a-half billion dollars. Violence now also became the key to unlimited self-enrichment.

The invasion of Tanzania was Amin's last act of madness. In retaliation, Tanzanian tanks, aided by Ugandan rebels, rolled into Kampala and defeated Africa's most notorious army. Obote's return to power, however, did not put an end to the violence. He came back as a 'wounded buffalo' according to one of his former aides, determined to take revenge on whoever had supported Amin.

In the early 1980s, an unknown third force emerged. A group of rebels led by the young revolutionary Yoweri Museveni and his brother, Salim Saleh, began an insurgency in the Luwero Triangle, an area in central Uganda. The rebels claimed they wanted to radically change a 'system of institutionalised violence which allows soldiers and armed agents to loot, rape and wipe out people and villages.' Not capable of stopping the rebels' advance, Obote resorted to murderous clearing operations, dubbed 'Operation Bonanza', in the Luwero Triangle. The International Committee of the Red Cross claimed that at least 300,000 people were killed during such operations.

In July 1985, Obote was removed by his own army. Commander Tito Okello took over and, for the first time, both political and military power came into the hands of an Acholi. Okello's regime lasted only six months. A peace agreement with the rebels fell apart after Okello called Museveni a 'snake,' whose fangs he would draw before crushing him. In January 1986, the rebels made their final push into the capital, Kampala. For the majority of the population, the long road to rehabilitation then began. But in the north a new cycle of violence started...

1

The lion has come up from his thicket, and the destroyer of the gentiles is on his way; he is gone forth from his place to make thy land desolate. (Jeremiah 4, 7)

Pitch-black was the night, as only African nights can be. The moon was hidden behind a thick blanket of clouds. Even the stars, that nowhere in the world shine so brightly as near the Equator, were covered in darkness. The rainy season was nearing its end. For months the monsoons had determined life in northern Uganda. They had turned the scorched plains into fertile fields and the roads into swamps. Again and again they had shaken the earth, ripped open the sky and flooded the huts.

That October night nature seemed to take a break. A chilly humidity rose from the steaming earth. Dozens of termites were jostling around the lamp in the parlour of St Mary's School in Aboke, a reputable girls' schools in northern Uganda. As usual after the rains, they emerged out of the blue, searching for the light, where they would burn their wings and die a slow, twisting death on the floor.

Sister Rachele, the deputy headmistress of the school, stared absentmindedly at the spectacle. She had a worried expression on her face. The Italian sister had been in Uganda for fourteen years. Fourteen years of war and anarchy. Yet, she hadn't regretted her decision for a moment. She was 19 when she gave up her job with the Italian electricity company to become a missionary. The Comboni mission first sent her to the United States, where she studied Biology, and then to Eritrea in the Horn of Africa to teach at a school in Asmara. Later she returned to Rome to study Medicine. But she broke off her studies after four years: she took the patients too much to heart and found it difficult to distinguish between her profession and her vocation. In fact, she longed for Africa, that continent of joy and sorrow where she felt both useful and at home. So she was delighted when she was sent

1

to Uganda in the early 1980s, where she became a Biology teacher at the school in Aboke.

She scanned the faces of the people sitting in the parlour. Sister Alba, the school's headmistress, looked troubled and worn out. With discipline and love, Alba had been striving to provide some of the country's best education. But tonight she was clearly indecisive. Also the two Ugandans, the Biology teacher and the Chemistry teacher, didn't know what to do. They had been loyal comrades, those two Alfreds. Even at the most precarious moments they had remained at their side. Once, after the government take-over, when soldiers were prowling around the area, they had protected the school all night, their pockets full of stones.

Sister Mathilde, the third Italian nun, looked at a loss. She had just arrived in Aboke, her suitcase was still unpacked, and she didn't seem to realise what was going on.

Sister Alba broke the silence. She jumped up and moved to the door.

'Haven't they come yet?' she called out to the watchman at the gate.

'No, sister, nobody came,' a voice replied from the darkness.

She sat back with a sigh. 'What are we going to do?' she turned to the others. 'Time is pressing. Shall we keep the girls here tonight or shall we take them to the village?'

'Taking them to the village this late could be more dangerous than keeping them here,' one of the teachers said.

There was another silence. Sister Rachele listened intently to the sounds outside. Did she hear footsteps? But there was only the monotonous chirping of crickets and the croaking of frogs. And faintly, in the distance, the ruffling of drums. It was the 9th of October. Independence Day was being celebrated in the neighbourhood. As if nothing was wrong.

She leaned back wearily. Events of the past twenty-four hours ran like a film through her head. Yesterday, she took home the headmistress of Icheme Girls' School after a meeting of the school's Board. Arriving there, she first heard rumours of rebels in the area. It had been a shock, more so as it came at a time when the school was left unprotected. The soldiers, who guarded the campus day and night, had been called back to the barracks for a check-up. She had immediately rushed to the army detachment at Iceme to see if the soldiers could be assigned back to the school. But the commander claimed he needed all his troops. He could only spare 19 homeguards, on condition that she would bring them back the next morning.

'Let us do this,' he suggested. 'As long as we cannot resume watching permanently, I will send my guards to you in the evening and you return them in the morning.'

As agreed, she had ferried the guards on the back of her pick-up to the school last night and had duly delivered them back to the barracks in the morning. But she would not leave before the commander had promised to send them back to the school in the afternoon.

'At six o'clock,' he said.

'No, six is too late. At four,' she insisted and he agreed.

She had proceeded to the barrracks at Loro, which had the only radio transmitter in the area. Could they send a message to the headquarters in Gulu and ask them to send reinforcements? she had asked the commander. 'Sixty soldiers. Otherwise we will close the school.' The commander had promised to do whatever he could. But his final words had followed her all the way back home. 'Sister,' he had said with a grave look, 'I know your school is a target.'

Her worries were confirmed when she reached the school late in the afternoon. The homeguards had not come. Worse, according to one of the teachers' their barracks had been attacked in the morning. He could not tell whether the army had been defeated.

'Let me go to the detachment at Otwal to get more information,' she told Alba. Otwal was north-west of Iceme, some 12 miles from the school. The road was muddy at this time of the year and only passable by bicycle. Alfred, the Biology teacher, accompanied her on the trip.

Communication, she reflected, was the biggest problem in northern Uganda. There were only a dozen telephone lines for the entire region, and a radio transmitter was too expensive. Moreover, radio messages could be listened to by anyone, including the rebels. Transmitting military information by radio was out of the question.

Yes, there had been fighting in Iceme, the commander at Otwal confirmed. According to his information, the rebels had been beaten back. It did not sound very convincing, though.

'Give me some of your soldiers,' she had pleaded. But he had reassured her. He would drive to Iceme himself to assess the situation. If there were any problems, he would come to the school and bring in reinforcements, even if it were at midnight.

Promises. So many promises. But when she arrived at the school shortly after eight, she could immediately tell from Alba's face that nobody had come. She still wanted to proceed to the police station at Aboke to find out what was happening. But Alba and the teachers had stopped her. It was too late.

The clock read a quarter past nine. For almost an hour, they had been sitting in the parlour, analysing the facts and considering the possibilities. In the classrooms, at the other side of the campus, the girls were studying in silence. Sister Alba had thought it better not to inform them so as not to create an unnecessary panic. Even in the past, when they had taken them to the village to spend the night in the houses of the workers, everything possible was done in order not to alarm them. It was only done out of precaution, they would tell them. They would return to the school the following morning.

Sister Rachele cut the knot. 'Maybe we should have confidence in the army,' she said. Alfred, the Biology teacher who had accompanied her on the bicycle trip, nodded. 'The soldiers in Iceme promised they would come. Those of Otwal promised they would come. Let us wait. They will come.'

Sister Alba looked intently at the two teachers. These were people from the area, she seemed to think. They could assess the situation better than she could. She looked around. 'Does everyone agree?' They all nodded. Sister Mathilde looked unsurely around and then joined the rest.

Everybody got up. Sister Alba went over to the kitchen to put the food out. Nineteen plates. After sending the girls to bed, she retired into the chapel. Rachele heard the tinkling of her rosary as she went to bed, feeling exhausted. 'God, let the school be spared,' she murmured before sinking into a restless sleep.

***

The Independence day party was in full swing and John Bosco was having a great time. He was a bachelor in his early 20s and parties like these were a welcome break in his life as a teacher at St Mary's. He liked the Italian sisters. They were courageous, he thought, coming all the way from Europe to live among the local people in this poor and desolate war-torn place.

'The rebels are coming!' The rumour spreading through the crowd hit John Bosco like a cold shower. His celebratory mood was suddenly gone. He looked at his watch. It was almost midnight.

'I have to go and warn the sisters,' he told his friends. But they tried to stop him. The soldiers who guarded the school could take him for a rebel and even shoot him if he turned up at the gate, they argued. After all, it was only a rumour. As usual, nothing would happen.

But John Bosco could not be persuaded. 'I'll go to the parish house and ask the fathers to take me there by car,' he whispered and before they could say anything, he was gone. Carefully, he made his way down the slippery path. As the music died away behind him, the unfolding silence scared him. God, how dark these nights could be in the rainy season! he thought. Exactly the kind of night the rebels favoured. With relief he saw the parish house looming up. He knocked at the gate. There was no reply. He knocked again.

'Fathers, open up. It's me, John Bosco, the teacher at St Mary's.'

But the place remained dark and silent. It occurred to him that they were probably afraid too. At times of insecurity people would not open for anyone. He had no choice but to go home, to his room at the teachers' quarters at the back of the campus which had a separate entrance. The place was quiet when he got there. He knocked at the doors of his fellow teachers. 'Wake up. The rebels are coming. We have to go and tell the sisters.'

But his colleagues tried to calm him.

'There is nothing to worry about,' they said. 'The situation is being closely monitored. Nothing will happen. Really.'

They promised to wake him if anything should happen. Not completely reassured, John Bosco went over to his room to try and catch some sleep.

***

Sister Rachele was woken up by a knock at the window. It was the watchman.

'Sister, the rebels are here.'

She looked at her watch. It was a quarter past two. Quickly she jumped out of bed and dressed up. Then she woke up Sister Alba. When the two came around the corner of the chapel a few minutes later, they stepped back in shock. The iron-wrought gate was lit up by a sea of dancing lights. They knew what this meant. When the Iceme mission was attacked some months ago, the Catholic father had described how one could recognise the rebels by their torch lights flickering in the night.

Without hesitating they turned around and rushed to the dormitories to urge the children to flee. But after a few steps they stopped again abruptly. The windows of the dormitories reflected the lights of numerous torches. 'They went straight to the dormitories,' Sister Rachele whispered. 'It is obvious, they want the girls. They didn't come to us first to ask for money or material things.'

The sisters looked at each other, not knowing what to do. Should they face the rebels or should they hide? The windows of the dormitories were barred, and the steel doors locked from inside. Without help, they judged, it was impossible for anyone to get in. If they confronted the rebels, however, they could be forced to urge the girls to open the doors. That danger, rather than fear for their lives, determined their decisionat that crucial moment. They ran back, woke up Sister Mathilde and threw themselves in the high elephant grass behind the convent storehouse.

Not much later a banging noise arose into the night. It reverberated over the swamps and the banana trees and the steaming fields. It drowned the chirping of crickets and the croaking of frogs. It seemed it would never stop. Lying in the wet grass, praying, one single thought went through Rachele's mind: 'I don't hear children's voices. They cannot get in. They are trying but they cannot get in.'

2

In spite of all this the people did not repent or renounce their sins, until they were carried off as plunder from their land.(Ecclesiasticus 48, 15)

'Will that banging never stop?' Ellen asked herself in despair. Like her classmates, the fourteen-year-old girl lay curled up under one of the iron bunk beds, frozen with fear. The torches cast flickering shadows on the walls. The floor was full of glass.

'Girls, open up!' voices outside shouted. But no one moved. A deadly silence hung over the dormitory. Everybody listened breathlessly to the loud, continuous banging. 'The door is bulletproof,' Ellen told herself in an attempt to stem her anxiety. 'They'll never manage.'

She tried to arrange her thoughts. Of course, she had heard the rumours. But, then, there had always been rumours. As long as she remembered, there had been talk of rebels. She had also noticed that the sisters looked nervous and concerned, but she had brushed it aside. It was Independence day. They had been singing and dancing and stuffing themselves with delicious food. For once, she did not want to think of the war. If there was any danger, the sisters would have taken them to the village, as they had done before. They had been sent to bed earlier than usual, but even that hadn't seemed strange after such a tiring day.

And then, suddenly, she had heard footsteps in the middle of the night. She automatically assumed it was the guards and dozed off again. But when a loud banging on the window broke the silence of the night and strange voices ordered the girls to open the door, she knew something was wrong. A moment later, the window panes were smashed. And in a split second, in the light of the flashes, she had seen the faces of her classmates, faces distorted with fear.

The atmosphere outside was growing more grim. One of the rebels now held a grenade through the broken window and threatened to blow up the entire building. A string of questions rushed through Ellen's head. Why had they not been taken to the village? Where were the sisters? And why weren't there any guards? But the questions became irrelevant when the next moment the window opened. With a deafening noise, the wall collapsed. One of the rebels climbed in and drew back the bolt of the door. Suddenly the dormitory was bathed in light and the rebels were all over the place. Heavily armed boys in military uniforms. They banged their guns on the iron beds.

'Come out, girls!'

Some of the students were dragged from under their beds. Ellen saw her neighbour being slapped over the head.

'Put on clothes that will help you to survive in the bush,' ordered a man who appeared to be in command. 'Dark clothes. Not white or red or yellow.'

The girls put on their school uniforms: a blue skirt and a blue sweater. Then they were tied to each other with ropes or with their own clothes, in groups of five or six, and pushed outside. One girl took advantage of the confusion. Quick as lightning, she swept through the dormitory and disappeared into the night. The rebels tried to pursue her but she was gone, swallowed by the darkness.

Ellen could not believe her eyes when she stood shivering in the chilly air of the night. Three-quarters of the school population was there: all the girls from Senior One to Senior Three, the 12- to 15-year-olds. They were tied together like prisoners, united in the same unknown destiny. Some girls were shaking uncontrollably. Ellen was astonished at her own calm. She had the feeling that she was not really experiencing this, as if somebody else had taken control of her body and the real she was looking on from above, coolly observing, devoid of all feelings and thoughts.

In this numb state, she let herself be led away over the wet playing field, past the grotto of the Virgin Mary, the convent and the dispensary. As if in a dream, she watched as the sisters' car was set on fire by the rebels. The commander screamed that he would throw them into the fire if they did not tell him where the sisters were, but his threats slid off her like drops of water. She did not blink when she walked through the opening in the fence and left the security of the campus behind. The future in front of her was as dark as the night. She told herself to take life step by step, without thinking ahead.

'Where are you taking us?' she heard herself ask one of the rebels. He told her to be brave. That they would come back.

Only then did Ellen realise that most of the rebels were themselves teenagers. Some were even younger than herself. She recognised some boys who were taken two months ago from Sir Samuel Baker School, another elite school in northern Uganda. Suddenly she felt sorry for those boys, her abductors, who were now holding guns instead of pens, and had become the terror rather than the pride of the north.

In front of the neighbouring primary school, a man lay motionless on the ground. He looked badly wounded. Ellen recognised him: he was a student at the nearby seminary. The next moment the line was brought to a halt. A second commander, a man with a distinct swollen upper lip, walked down the line, scrutinising them one by one. He picked out some smaller girls and ordered them to be untied. A girl with a paralysed hand was also released. With a twinge in the chest, Ellen watched them leave. She was not among the lucky ones.

They were ordered to continue moving. But after only a few steps she heard a loud whistle. Ellen knew that sound. It was the warning signal the villagers used when the rebels were coming. The next moment a gunshot rang out in the night. Ellen threw herself down at the side of the road for cover. But she was hampered by her tied hands and slipped in the mud.

In the confusion that followed, some girls managed to free themselves and escape. The commander was furious. His face was distorted with anger when at the next homestead he ordered the rebels to form two lines, facing each other. The Aboke girls were told to pass through the lines, while they were being kicked and beaten from both sides. But Ellen did not feel anything. She had left her body and underwent the punishment in total apathy. She had found the trick to survive. Whatever it took, survive she would.

***

Norman stared blankly in front of him as he marched behind his commander, Mariano Ocaya Lagira. The machine gun weighed heavily on his shoulders. He tried to keep it steady as they waded through a deep swamp. The boy was almost 14 but he was so small, he looked no older than 12. His face displayed the grim look of a rebel. But inside he felt sad, as sad as the girls he was guarding. They looked really nice. In a normal life, he would probably have fancied some of them. But life hadn't been normal for a long time.

He took a deep breath. It was almost two years since he himself had been abducted from his village near Gulu. The day of his abduction would stick in his mind forever. It was New Year's Day and the rebels had attacked his village. He had run with his uncle and little brother to one side, while his parents had fled to the other side. When they came out of hiding in the evening, they had walked straight into the rebels' hands. He and his brother were captured and walked at gunpoint to the rebel base. The next morning his brother was released, while he was taken on the long journey to the north, to a world too gruesome for anyone to imagine.

A few days ago, when they passed through his village, Norman had been reminded again of that awful day. 'Come on, show me your house,' his group leader, Captain Ojara, had spurred him. But Norman had instantly been on his guard. It could be a trick to kill his parents, so that he would have nobody to return to and he would have to spend the rest of his life with the rebels. He had seen it happen to other abducted children before, especially those who had cried out for their mothers.

'I heard the government soldiers march in that direction,' he had quickly replied. 'We might run into them.'

The trick had worked and Ojara had not insisted. But Norman felt sick and totally confused when they left his village behind. It was as if it already belonged to a different life.

He turned around and checked on the line of girls tied together. Some were crying. 'If I were not forced, I would never do this,' he told himself. 'But if I don't obey, I'll be killed.' He was glad he did not have to go to the dormitories himself. He had been spared the scenes there. His task had been to keep watch at the gate. The school had been covered in darkness when they got there. One group was sent to the centre where the music came from. The second, led by B.M. Oyet, was to attack the mission.

In fact, Norman had suspected it for some time. Since that cryptic message on the radio, he had known that something big was going to happen. 'I will go and get what you told me, his commander had said in the coded language the rebels used. And the voice at the other side had replied: 'Standing by.'

For two days they had been steadily advancing towards their target. On the way, they had met more resistance than expected. At one point, they had even run into an ambush of the government troops. But they had managed to defeat them, killing several soldiers and taking most of their guns. One of his fellow rebels had died in that battle and a second one, whom they were now carrying along, got seriously wounded.

An unusually large group of rebels had been selected for the Aboke raid, some 150 men in all. After all, the top leader himself had ordered the operation. He would stand by and follow events over the radio. It could not go wrong.

3

How glorious he was when he raised his hand and brandished his sword against cities! Never before had a man made such a stand, for he was fighting the Lord's battles. (Ecclesiasticus 46, 2-3)

A thin line of light peeped on the horizon. Then, as if an invisible hand pulled away the curtain of the night, morning broke, spreading its glow and warmth over the dew-drenched earth. The world suddenly looked more friendly to Sister Rachele, less hostile.

One by one, the sisters got up. They stretched their stiff limbs and got rid of the dirt from their dresses. For hours, they had been lying in the damp grass. From their hiding places they had seen the flames coming from the garage. Later they had heard the church bells ring, assuming it was the rebels who were retreating frustrated. No, they had no doubt the attackers had left empty-handed.

Suddenly, in the twilight, they saw some girls running towards them.

'Children, are you all there?' Sister Alba called out.

But the first girl to reach them burst into tears.

'Sister, they've taken all of us', she stammered. 'From Senior One to Senior Three. We were later released because we were too small.'

The sisters looked at each other in disbelief. Then they rushed to the dormitories where they found the first block, of Senior Four to Six, untouched.

'Girls, are you there?' Sister Rachele called out.

It took some time before anyone answered. At last, hesitantly, as if to make sure it was safe, the girls came out, wailing and weeping. They had seen everything through the windows, they said. Their younger schoolmates had been tied with ropes and sweaters and taken away in a long line. No, they couldn't understand why they were left alone. The rebels hadn't even tried to enter their dormitory. Sister Rachele watched the building which stood separate from the other blocks. Suddenly she caught sight of the corn cobs that lay drying in front.

12

'The maize,' she pointed out to Alba. 'The rebels must have thought it was a storehouse!'

Followed by the students, the sisters worked their way to the other dormitories. The path was littered with slippers, clothes, and other possessions left by the children. The windows were shattered and the bars bent, but nowhere could they spot an opening big enough for a human being to enter. How did they get in? Sister Rachele wondered. Only when they reached the entrance to the two dormitories, did she understand. Next to the metal door gaped a huge hole. The rebels had simply smashed the wall around the window and lifted out the entire frame.

'What about the Senior One dormitory?' Sister Alba asked. 'How did they get in there?'

There was a moment of silence. Then one of the younger students came forward and explained that a girl got frightened when the rebels threatened to throw in a hand grenade.

'She got up and opened the door from the inside.'

Sister Alba shook her head in astonishment. Rachele just stood there, staring at the broken wall. The persistence with which the wall was smashed seemed to invoke the same kind of determination in her. She turned to her superior.

'Alba, I'm going to follow them.'

The headmistress did not hesitate a moment.

'Go, with God's blessing'.

Sister Rachele hurried to her room to change. Only then did she discover that the mission had been looted. Bedsheets and radio sets were missing. Sister Mathilde's unpacked suitcase was left on the lawn; probably because it was too heavy to carry. The kitchen and the dispensary too had been broken into. Sister Rachele didn't take much notice of this as she rushed to the administration building at the other side of the school grounds to get what she thought could save her girls.

Crossing the campus, she ran into John Bosco. The teacher had been woken up by the sound of wailing, discovering that all his colleagues had fled. Tears rolled down her cheeks as Sister Rachele broke the news to him.

13

'How many pupils are missing?' he asked in horror.

'One hundred and fifty-two.'

'And the soldiers?'

'They did not come.'

He cursed and wanted to tell her what had happened the previous night. But Sister Rachele interrupted him.

'Bosco, will you come with me?'

He immediately understood what she meant. At the same time he knew it was a crazy idea. Those rebels were killers, striking down anybody who came their way in cold blood. Yet, to his own surprise, he didn't feel any fear.

'Sister, let us go,' he said bravely. 'Let us go and die for our girls.'

Rachele quickly entered her office and opened the safe. She took out Shs 700,000 and put the money in her bag. As she came out, she felt somebody grabbing her. It was a student of Senior One. The girl clung to her, her body shaking with sobs.

'Sister, they raped me,' she stuttered.

It was too much for Rachele.

'Alba, take care of this child,' she said and together with John Bosco, she left the school.

***

They followed a track of sweet wrappers and empty soda bottles, remnants of the things the rebels had looted from the school store. When they left the main road and walked over a dirt track, the footprints guided them. They walked in silence, along banana plantations, tangled thickets and swampy fields. Every now and then Sister Rachele's sandals would slip in the mud. At one time, when they waded through a swamp, the water almost reached her waist. Her dress got soaked and looked all dirty, but that was the least of her worries.

John Bosco suddenly turned to her, a worried expression on his face.

'Sister, put your feet where I put mine. The rebels tend to plant mines when they retreat, to stop the army from following them'. She carefully placed her feet in his tracks. But the thought of seeing this young man stepping onto a mine and being blown up in front of her, made her break into a cold sweat.

The elephant grass on both sides of the path was obstructing their sight. They had no idea how far ahead the rebels were. There was nobody to ask either. The family homesteads they passed through were deserted. All inhabitants had fled from those mysterious rebels, who had been around for almost ten years. The Movement of the Holy Spirit, they used to call themselves at the end of the 1980s. Later they changed their name to God's Salvation Army, and finally settled for the Lord's Resistance Army or LRA.

They also changed leadership three times. First there had been Alice Lakwena, the 'witch of the north' as she was called, a charismatic woman who believed she was the reincarnation of the Holy Spirit. She had led hundreds of young men to their deaths by telling them that the stones they threw at the enemy would explode like grenades and the oils smeared on their bodies would cause bullets to bounce harmlessly off their chests.

When her magic had faded and her army had thinned out considerably, her father, Severino, who called himself 'God the Father,' took over. His movement was a poor imitation of his daughter's and he had to use force to recruit followers. They too perished in great numbers, mowed down by bullets while they marched to the frontline, cheering and clapping.

Since then their cousin, Joseph Kony, had taken charge. Little was known about this man except that he was in his mid-thirties and had never finished primary school. His political programme was as obscure as it was simple: overthrow the government in Uganda and then rule the country by the Ten Commandments.

John Bosco abruptly stopped. He signalled to Sister Rachele to be quiet. She could faintly hear voices coming their way. They waited until a group of villagers emerged, returning from hiding.

'Have you seen the girls?' Rachele called out.

One of the men nodded. 'They are marching with the rebels in the direction of Otwal. They must be a few hours ahead.'

They quickened their pace. It was past ten o'clock. They had been walking for three hours. Fortunately, Rachele was a good walker.

Although she was nearing fifty, she could walk for hours without getting tired. Again they heard the sound of people, but it was different from the first time. In fact, it sounded like wailing.

They hurried to the next homestead, where they found two women weeping in front of a hut. The rebels passed and took her daughter, the younger of the two stuttered.

'How long ago was that?' Sister Rachele asked.

'They must be at the rock called Omiri.'

John Bosco briefly explained what they wanted to do.

'Can I come along?' the young woman begged, brushing away her tears. He looked questioningly at Sister Rachele.

'Sure,' she replied quickly. 'Let her come with us.'

They walked behind each other, in one line: John Bosco in front, the woman in the middle and Rachele at the rear. The sun was almost on top of their heads now. Sister Rachele felt her dress stick to her back. A rocky hill emerged in the distance.

'Omiri,' the woman pointed.

It would make a good observation post, Sister Rachele thought. They had just started climbing when her attention was caught by something on the ground. She bent over and picked up a pair of slippers and an identity card of one of her girls. At the same time, John Bosco, higher up, called her.

'Sister, the rebels are there.'

She rushed to his position at the top of the hill. At the other side of the valley, hardly 200 metres away, she saw a long line of people climbing the next hill.

'What shall we do?' she asked the teacher.

He looked at her for a moment, doubtful. Then he repeated bravely: 'Let us go and die for our girls.'

His words encouraged her. She raised her hand and waved. Somebody on the other side had noticed them. He also put up his hand and shouted something which she couldn't understand.

'Sister, he is telling us not to wave,' Bosco said. 'He is telling us to come forward with our hands up.'

They went down the hill, their hands in the air. The path took a sharp turn so that for a while the grass hid them from the rebels. The next moment they were staring into dozens of gun barrels. The rebels, some thirty of them, were standing in two lines, their guns pointed at them. They were all wearing boots and army uniforms, and they carried heavy, modern weapons. Bullets were hanging like garlands around their necks. But it was the look in their eyes that frightened Sister Rachele most: looks as cold as ice.

4

And when it was day, he called unto him his disciples: and of them
he chose twelve, whom also he named apostles. (St Luke 6, 13)

Norman saw her coming with her hands up, that small *muzungu* nun
with her soiled veil and dirty dress, accompanied by two local people.
He stood in the middle of the line. 'If they are followed by soldiers,
we'll shoot them, he heard his commander say. The boy tried to keep
a straight face,' his eyes blank and devoid of emotions. It was this
pose that kept him going, that made him survive in the bush. But the
questions were swirling in his head. What was the matter with her?
Did that *muzungu* know what she was doing? Everywhere they passed,
people ran away from them and here was somebody – a white woman
too – who walked undaunted towards them! At the same time, he
thought she was brave, braver than any civilian he had come across in
the last two years.

   He looked at the girls. They had been made to sit along the path on
the slope of the hill and told to keep quiet. The visitors were now
standing right in front of the storm troops. A strained silence hung
over the valley. Norman glanced at his commander. He knew one order
could mow this woman down. They had killed and maimed people for
less: for riding a bicycle, or for tending their fields on Fridays. The
sister started talking. He could not make out what she was saying. He
kept his eyes fixed on Lagira. The man felt clearly uneasy. This was a
situation he was not prepared for. As the conversation continued, his
features softened. Now, there was even the hint of a smile on his face.
Norman took a deep breath. The danger was over.

***

'I am the sister of Aboke. I would like to talk to your commander.'
   Sister Rachele spoke softly and with caution. She knew it was now
a matter of saying the right words at the right time. She had clearly

sensed the tension in the air and the hostility in the faces in front of her. One wrong word, one careless movement, she knew, could be fatal.

The man with the swollen upper lip came forward.

'I am the commander.'

She nodded in greeting, forcing a smile. But he immediately made it clear he was the one to ask the questions.

'Do you speak Acholi?'

'I lived in Gulu for some time. I know a bit of Lango.'

'Where were you when we came to the mission?'

She hesitated, but only for an instant.

'I wasn't there. I took Sister Alba to Lira because she was sick. When I came back this morning and found out what had happened.., I mean when I didn't find the girls...., I said to myself: let me follow those people. I'm sure they will give them back to me.'

He peered at her with half-closed eyes.

'You are deceiving me.'

She swallowed. 'Commander, I came to ask you to give me the girls.' Pointing at her bag, she added: 'I even brought some money.' The commander ordered one of his aides to check the bag. The boy grabbed the bag and took out a pen, a piece of paper, a crucifix and a bundle of bank notes.

'Put everything back and return it to her,' he told the soldier.

Then he turned to the sister.

'We don't want money.'

Rachele looked up at him.

'Please, commander, let me have the girls.'

He scrutinised her for a long time. Then suddenly his face turned friendly. 'Don't worry, sister, I will give you the girls.'

She sighed with relief. The certainty that she could talk to this man gave her confidence. And talk he did, as if he had known her for years. How they could move fast as lightning through the bush. And how they had recently attacked Karuma, the bridge over the Nile, and killed a lot of soldiers.

'This walkie-talkie we took from them', he grinned. 'We are not as stupid as people say we are.'

Then he caught sight of the woman from the village who had accompanied them and his face suddenly darkened.

'That woman has been disturbing us,' he snorted, waving his finger at her. 'Get out or we could do something very bad to you.' The woman stepped back in fear, then she turned around and fled.

He signalled to his troops to start moving. Rachele told John Bosco to stay close to the commander. Together they climbed the hill. She had taken her rosary from her pocket and fiddled with the beads.

'What are you doing?' the commander asked.

'I'm praying that you may give me the girls.'

'Don't worry,' he reassured her, 'I will give you the girls.'

Another officer had joined them. He also pulled out his rosary and smiled. 'With this one we are going to win'.

At last, from the top of the hill, she saw her girls. They were seated along the path, in one long line. The rebels were positioned in between them. She tried to smile at them but nobody responded. Sister Rachele and John Bosco were taken to a second commander, seated under a tree in the valley. As they passed the line, one of the girls burst into tears. It was Jenny, the headgirl. Sister Rachele noticed that her dress was torn. The commander patted her on the head. 'Don't cry,' he soothed.

The second commander looked bigger and younger than the first one. Rachele repeated the purpose of their coming. He examined her and then asked: 'Where was the parish priest when we came?'

Careful not to upset him, she simply answered: 'He was not at home.' He seemed to be satisfied with the answer and got up. The first commander yelled an order to move. The girls scrambled to their feet and the long caravan was set in motion.

Sister Rachele made sure that she didn't move an inch from the commander's side. The guards marched up and down, making the girls hurry on in a brutal way. The pace was fast. A wounded rebel was pulled along on a makeshift stretcher. Only then did Sister Rachele notice that most of the rebels were children themselves. Some were very small.

'You can talk to your girls,' the commander encouraged her.

She tried to start a conversation but nobody replied. She turned to the commander instead. 'You can ask me anything. Do you want medicine? Food? Anything.'

He shook his head. 'We don't need anything,' he replied. 'Don't worry, sister, you will get your girls.'

They stopped at a deserted market place near the railway at Achokara. The commander ordered his troops to put down the goods. He got seated on a trunk and told the visitors to sit next to him. One of his aides immediately got busy installing the solar panel.

'We are going to charge the batteries so that I can communicate with my superior,' he explained.

Then he ordered the Aboke girls to be separated from the rest of the captives. Only then did Sister Rachele realise that there were more abducted children. She suddenly felt guilty that she had only come for her girls.

'Only the students of Aboke on this side', the commander shouted as if guessing her thoughts. 'If you allow anybody else to hide in your group, I won't let anybody go.'

Sister Rachele signalled to the girls to be quiet, to do as they were told. The next moment they were all down on the ground. The rebels had noticed the helicopter before she had. The commander had screamed an order and everyone had dispersed. Some were lying in the tall grass. Rachele was hiding under the edge of a thatched roof. She was told to pull off her veil, in order not to be seen. The helicopter gunship circled over the market place. It was obvious that the soldiers up there had spotted them. But what could they do? Rachele wondered. How could they distinguish the rebels from the children?

When at last the chopper lifted itself and took off, the commander ordered everybody to collect the goods and to get moving. Rachele rushed over to him.

'Please, leave me here with the girls. We might interfere with your movements.'

'We move!' he snapped.

They crossed the railway and followed a track at the other side, edged by elephant grass. The sound of gunshots was drawing nearer.

21

The next moment bullets were flying over their heads. They threw themselves into the grass. Some pupils covered Sister Rachele with their bodies to protect her. 'Probably the soldiers of Otwal,' John Bosco whispered next to her. He had been ordered to take off his white shirt and was now wearing a blue sweater of one of the girls. Some students too had been ordered to remove their blouses. When there was a pause in the shooting, they were pushed forward again, like a herd of cattle.

'Hurry up!' yelled a girl with a black skirt, and she beat them with the butt of her rifle. Bosco received a blow on the back.

'Where is the commander?' Sister Rachele asked one of the guards. 'Tell him I want to talk to him.'

After a while, he came over. 'Why don't you leave me here with the girls?' she pleaded again. 'We are only a burden to you.'

'Get moving,' he interrupted her.

The rattling sound returned. Again they were forced to hide, and to get moving as soon as the helicopter had turned away. It seemed to go on forever: hiding, moving, hiding, moving. At one point, they were told to cover their heads with cassava leaves and walk on under the rotating helicopter.

The sun was low when the army finally gave up the pursuit. They stopped at what seemed to be a camp site, a large open space surrounded by banana trees and some huts. The commander got seated and removed his boots. A woman immediately rushed over to bring him a pair of slippers. Then she spread a plastic sheet on the floor. With a flick of his hand, he invited Sister Rachele and John Bosco to sit next to him. The Aboke girls were seated at some distance opposite them, so that they could see but not hear each other. The other captives were put behind them. The commander got up and inspected the last group.

'You are the one who gave the alarm,' Sister Rachele heard him say angrily. He yelled an order to his troops and they started beating the culprit fiercely. Sister Rachele did not look back. She only heard the blows coming down, and the agonised cry of the girl.

A boy knelt beside her. 'Sister, please, tell the commander I am a seminarian so that he allows me to come with you.'

The scene didn't escape the commander's attention.

'What does he want?'

'He says he is a seminarian. Could you let him go with us?'

He looked at the boy for a moment. 'We are all seminarians here,' he replied and he sent him back to the group.

With a satisfied look on his face, he leaned back. 'Have I told you that my name is Mariano Ocaya?' he suddenly turned to Rachele.

'And my name is Sister Rachele'

'Do you have a picture of Our Lady?'

The question surprised her. She took the crucifix from her bag and gave it to him. He held it for a while in both hands and then put it in his breast pocket.

She took advantage of this confidential moment.

'Mariano, why don't we stop this war? Our people have suffered enough.'

He bent towards her. 'We will stop this war when Museveni agrees to rule the country by the Ten Commandments.' His face took on a conspiratorial look. 'We came to the school with a mission. If we had found a priest, we would not have done what we did.'

He called the woman who had brought the slippers. She reappeared, carrying a piece of soap and a basin filled with water.

'Go and bathe,' he told Rachele.

She looked at Bosco, puzzled.

'He is telling you to go and wash,' the teacher repeated.

She got up and followed the woman to a place where banana leaves were spread on the ground. The basin was left on top of the leaves and the woman disappeared. Rachele looked around, uncertain what she was supposed to do. Some guards stood by, watching her. She let the water splash over her face. Then she washed her hands and her feet. After a while the woman came back, carrying a yellow dress and a white petticoat. 'Change,' she said with a straight face.

Sister Rachele thanked her but declined. 'I have my nun's habit.'

But the woman insisted.

'Thank you but I am a sister,' she said more firmly. 'Please, let me keep my own dress.'

The woman relented and took her back to the commander. A bench had now been placed for John Bosco and herself. As she got seated, she immediately sensed something had changed.

'Mariano, it is getting late. Will you now give me the girls?'

But he shook his head.

'Sister, he is not going to give them all,' John Bosco said in a low voice.

She turned to the commander in alarm.

'Mariano, please, give me all the girls.'

He bent forward and with his finger he formed the number 139 in the sand.

'The girls are 139.'

His fingers wrote 109. 'I will give you back 109.'

Then he wrote 30. 'I keep thirty.'

Sister Rachele looked at him, baffled. Then she knelt down in front of him.

'Keep me here,' she pleaded, her hand resting on the crucifix in his breast pocket. 'Let the children go but keep me here.'

He gestured her to get up. 'I keep thirty,' he repeated. 'But if Kony agrees, the others will be released tomorrow.'

'Take me to Kony. Let me talk to him.'

He shook his head. 'You cannot talk to him.' He paused and then added: 'You can only write to him.'

She opened her bag, took out pen and paper and wrote in her poor Lango:

Dear Mr Kony,

I am Sister Rachele of Aboke. I ask you kindly to give me the thirty girls that are remaining with your commander Mariano. Thank you very much.

She showed it to John Bosco to read. He nodded in approval. Then she handed it to the commander. He read it too, put it in his pocket and stood up.

24

'Come, go and write down the names of the girls who will stay behind.'

He led her to a group of girls seated at the back. She realised there and then that the thirty had already been selected. She had no idea which criteria had been used. As soon as the thirty girls got sight of her, they started crying and screaming. The commander's face turned savage. He lifted his hand and the surrounding rebels instantly threw themselves on the girls. They beat and kicked them viciously and jumped on top of them with their gumboots. The girls curled themselves up, trying to avert the blows with their hands and arms. Sister Rachele stared at the scene in anguish. Tears were rolling down her face. Never before had she felt so utterly powerless, at the mercy of this one man. The girls stopped screaming and at one sign, the beating too stopped.

The girls now looked at her, their eyes wide with terror.

'Sister, will you come back tonight to bring us our bed sheets?' Charlotte asked.

'Sister, I have my period. Can you bring me pads?' Grace whispered.

'Sister, I have asthma and my mother is sick. Tell him!' Janet insisted.

'Sister, tonight they might rape us,' Justine said.

Others said nothing. They just stared at her with sad, fearful eyes. She knew there and then that these looks would haunt her for the rest of her life.

It was too much. She turned to the commander and knelt in front of him, her hands folded. 'Mariano, please, give them all back to me. Keep me here instead.'

He exploded in rage. 'If you do that once more, I will not give you any!' he screamed and he ran off.

Rachele quickly pulled herself together. She got up and started taking down the names. But the paper in her hand trembled and she found it hard to write. Angela stood up and took the pen and paper.

'Sister, I will write our names,' she said quietly.

The commander called Sister Rachele over. Reaching the place where John Bosco was, she saw that tea and biscuits had been prepared for them. Other officers were there too. They chatted away as if this was an ordinary tea gathering. But Sister Rachele could not concentrate on anything that was being said. She just stared in front of her, cradling the cup in her hands. The only thing she noticed was that the tea was sweet, sweeter than any she had ever tasted.

After tea-break the commander clapped his hands. 'Prayer time!' From everywhere the rebels swarmed to the open space. They knelt down in long, orderly lines. The commander walked over to a chair in front of the crowd and took out his rosary. The prayer was very short, but long enough for Sister Rachele to count about 200 rebels.

'Now go and say goodbye to your girls,' Mariano said when he returned to her.

She walked over to the other side. Angela handed her the piece of paper. One by one Sister Rachele read the names of those who had to stay behind and looked for their faces. But someone was missing.

'Janet is not there,' Angela whispered.

'Where is she?'

'She went to hide in the other group.'

Rachele was aware of the awful dilemma she was facing. If she left with Janet, she would have saved another child. But if the commander discovered that someone was missing, he could become angry again and keep everybody.

'Angela, go and call Janet.'

Janet emerged, trembling. She knelt down next to the sister.

Rachele embraced her. 'Janet, girl don't do this,' she whispered. 'You put all your friends in danger.'

And the girl replied softly: 'Sister, I will not do it again.'

Sister Rachele said a last prayer with the 30 girls. Then she told them to get their friends' sweaters for the cold nights. Rachele handed her rosary to Jenny, the head girl. 'Take good care of the other children,' she said. And to the rest of the group: 'Girls, when we leave, don't look at us.'

As she returned to John Bosco, she noticed something was wrong. The officers were discussing fiercely.

'Sister, they are considering not letting us go,' John Bosco told her in an agitated way. 'They say it is too late.'

Rachele vowed not to let this happen. These people could change their minds at any time. After their radio contact with Kony, they might even decide to keep them all.

'Mariano, it is getting dark. Give me a torch,' she broke off the discussion. He sent one of his soldiers for a torch. Then she turned to the students.

'Girls, the commander is letting you go home, so let us thank him.'

The girls bowed and murmured: 'Thank you.'

'If Mr Kony agrees, tomorrow your friends will return home as well,' she went on.

Mariano now also faced the group.

'Did I harass you?' he asked.

'No,' the girls answered in one voice.

'Did I harass the sister?'

'No.'

'So next time when I come to your school, don't run away.'

He insisted that they take a guide with them. And then, in a sudden impulse, he called a little girl from the other group of captives. 'You can also take home this girl.'

Sister Rachele grabbed the child's hand. She was hardly ten years old. Then the sister and the rebel leader said goodbye to each other. The guards too rose to salute her. Without looking back, in one long line, they left the camp.

5

And thou shall anoint Aaron and his sons, and consecrate them, that they may minister unto me in the priest's office. (Exodus 30, 30)

Ellen didn't look back when her friends walked away. She knew why the sister had told them not to. If they watched them leave, they might cry again and get another beating. Not that it would have made any difference to her. She still felt oddly detached, as if her body didn't belong to her.

Unlike her fellow students, she hadn't cried all day. She hadn't stirred when the sister arrived. 'If you cry, you will stay with us in the bush,' the commander had warned. She hadn't been afraid when the helicopter was hovering above them. They were told not to look up, but she secretly looked up, hoping that the soldiers would see her and fire and that would be the end. She hadn't blinked when she was the fourth girl selected to stay behind. 'Jesus also chose 12 apostles,' the rebels had explained. 'In the same way, we select thirty: 30 angels.' Neither had she cried when the sister came to register their names. She had only stared at her, resignedly. Whatever was to follow, it left her cold.

Her thoughts were interrupted by loud voices. 'We should not have released those 109!' one of the officers screamed. 'Even the sister we should have kept.'

The commander with the swollen lip didn't reply. He only selected some rebels and sent them after the sister. Ellen watched them leave, guns dangling from their shoulders.

The Aboke girls were ordered to move to where the other captives were. Ellen counted about 60 of them. The commander was standing in front of the group, addressing them. Like all newcomers, he said, they had to be anointed, so as to be blessed by the Holy Spirit. With oil from the sheanut tree, the rebels then smeared a sign of the cross on their foreheads, their shoulders and their chests.

'Now you are soldiers of the movement and you can eat together with the others,' they were told. A stolen goat was slaughtered and roasted but neither Ellen nor her friends had any appetite.

After the meal, they were divided into groups of five or six and assigned to different units. These were like small families: a commander, his wives and the children-recruits. The wives, who were also carrying guns, had to ensure that none of the newcomers ran away.

'If one of you escapes, the other recruits of your unit will be punished,' the commander warned, 'and that punishment could be death.'

The Aboke girls were not allowed to talk to each other or to speak English. That would be considered as plotting an escape.

Then they were sent to a thatched hut for the last night they were allowed to spend together. But the hut was too small for all of them. They tried to settle as comfortably as they could. Ellen was seated in the corner, with her back against the wall and her knees pulled up. Only now did she feel how tired she was. No wonder, they had been walking all day. Slowly she dozed off.

She woke up with a start in the middle of the night, at first not knowing where she was. Then with a shock, she remembered everything. The moon had appeared behind the clouds and lit up the tiny place. She looked around at her friends who were crammed in the hut like sardines in a tin. Suddenly, she craved for home, for her father, a prominent schoolteacher, and her mother who spared no effort to raise their ten children. How would they react to her disappearance? She had been the pride of the family, because she studied at St Mary's and had been among the brightest girls of the school. She had wanted to be a lawyer. The tears welled up. She felt unable to stop them. And for the first time since their abduction she cried, her body shaking violently.

'Ellen, don't cry,' the girls around her whispered. 'They are going to beat you.'

But she couldn't control herself. It was as if the dam of courage she had hedged around her heart had finally collapsed, releasing the tide of emotions she had stemmed for so long.

***

Sister Rachele gratefully looked up at the moon. Finally, some light. Not that it made her any wiser. The fields and bushes around her looked as unfamiliar as they had in the dark. She had no idea where they were, nor if they were going in the right direction.

Initially, all had gone well. The rebel escort had put them on the right track and left them after some 200 metres. She had taken over the lead, while John Bosco took up the rear. With the help of the torch and the girls' directions, they had crossed forests, fields and pastures. But suddenly the path was gone. 'Lost,' she shrugged as John Bosco came running with a frown. He took over the torch and followed the direction by instinct, but he couldn't find the path either. They halted at the next homestead to ask for directions, only to discover that all the huts were empty.

'The people must have been alarmed by our footsteps,' he turned to Sister Rachele. 'They probably think we are the rebels returning. There are too many of us.' He pondered for a while.

'Why don't you hide with the girls, while I look for help?' he then suggested. 'On my own, I'll have a better chance.'

Sister Rachele didn't like the idea of staying behind with the girls, but she realised she had no choice. They selected a large, newly built hut and all the girls entered.

'Don't be long,' she called after the teacher.

They squeezed into the house, all 111 of them. Sister Rachele placed herself at the entrance, facing the door. The place was too small really, but she didn't want anybody to stay outside. She felt exhausted. The moonlight peeped through the window. She suddenly thought she saw the flashes of torches. She gestured to the girls to be quiet, not to move. Did she hear footsteps outside? She hadn't been afraid all day but now she was overcome by sheer panic. Suppose that another group of rebels found them here? Or suppose they had moved in circles and were back at the camp. She kept her eyes fixed at the door. Whoever would attempt to enter would first have to deal with her. In a way as acute as irrational, she sensed that there was danger. Great danger. What was keeping Bosco?

***

'I have to find the local councillor,' John Bosco told himself. He regretted he had to remove his white shirt. With the blue sweater of one of the girls he could more easily be taken for a rebel. It was the second night he was wandering around, looking for help, but there was nobody to turn to. He heard voices coming his way. He decided to hide at the side of the road and wait until the people had come close enough, so that they would not run away at the first sight of him. But when he jumped onto the road, the villagers dashed off as if they had seen a ghost.

'Don't run away. It's me. I am one of you,' he called after them but they were already gone.

Like a thief in the night, he sneaked up to the next homestead. But again most people took to their heels when he emerged. Only an old man stayed behind, seated in front of a hut.

'I am guarding the body of my dead wife,' he told John Bosco. 'We wanted to bury her today but the rebels arrived so we couldn't finish the grave.' He insisted that Bosco greet the corpse.

One by one the mourners came out of hiding. As John Bosco related his story, he could read the disbelief on the faces of his listeners.

'Can somebody take me to the local councillor?' he finally asked.

The villagers looked at each other, clearly not knowing what to make out of this stranger. At last two boys offered to guide him, on condition that they first saw the sister and the girls. John Bosco agreed and the three set off.

They walked in silence. The teacher sensed that his companions didn't trust him. It got worse when he got lost. The first hut he led them to appeared to be empty. He ran over to a second one. Wrong again.

'Do you know a newly built hut?' he asked helplessly.

There was now both fear and hostility in the boys' eyes. 'We'll try a last one,' one of them warned. 'If we don't find those people, we'll leave you.'

31

It was with relief that he heard Sister Rachele's voice.

'Bosco, are you there?'

'It's me, sister.'

'Just in time,' she sighed when he pushed the door open.

Two girls had fainted from lack of air. They were carried outside, where John Bosco started fanning them with his sweater. The escorts changed instantly, becoming friendly and helpful now. After everyone had recovered, they guided them to the councillor's house. They crossed the railway at Achokara. Had they really walked all that far? Sister Rachele wondered.

The councillor must have been informed of their coming as he was waiting for them. Immediately he put his two houses at their disposal. Beds of papyrus were spread on the floor and the man moved up and down to the bore-hole to fetch water. It was after midnight when everybody was settled for the night. Sister Rachele found it hard to catch some sleep. Tomorrow, she knew, a new nightmare was awaiting her: facing the parents of the 30 girls she had had to leave behind.

***

In the pale light of dawn, they all stood dressed and ready to leave. The girls had washed at the bore-hole and were now eager to get home. Sister Rachele thanked the councillor effusively and they began the last part of the journey. The morning air smelled fresh and new. The sky had cleared and the sun felt warm and reassuring. Sister Rachele had told the girls to walk quietly so as not to frighten the villagers. But the caravan didn't pass unnoticed. Everywhere people came running out of their houses. At the sight of the children, they started clapping and cheering. The news of the abduction had obviously spread like wild fire. But when Sister Rachele told them that she had to leave 30 girls behind, their joy gave way to expressions of grief and empathy.

A big crowd had gathered at Otwal railway station. One of the teachers of St Mary's was there too.

'Go and inform Sister Alba that we are coming,' Rachele told him.

Then she sent some onlookers for sodas and biscuits, which she paid for with the money that was still in her bag. It was their first meal in almost two days. They had just started moving again when a Land-Rover appeared in the distance. Sister Alba, at last! Rachele felt the tension fall like a heavy burden from her shoulders. The car stopped in front of them. There was no time for any explanation. The weakest girls were loaded onto the vehicle. Rachele also got in.

'The tractor with trailer is on its way to collect the others,' Alba said.

From a distance, Rachele saw the parents coming, on bicycles, motorcycles and pick-ups. She got out. The paper with the names of the girls was trembling in her hands. Barbara's mother was the first to reach them. The woman jumped from the motorcycle and looked at her hopefully.

'Is my Barbara there?'

Rachele's eyes filled with tears.

'She's not here,' one of the girls shouted from the back of the car. In alarm, the woman turned to Sister Rachele, but she couldn't utter a word. The next moment Barbara's mother rolled herself in the grass, constantly calling the name of her daughter. Other parents arrived and the scenes were heartbreaking. Some embraced their daughters, overwhelmed with joy. Others who didn't find their children, screamed in agony. Sister Rachele stared at the scenes silently, tears rolling down her face.

'Come', Sister Alba softly pulled her sleeve. 'Let us go home.'

More parents were waiting at the school gate. Again the same scenes. Alba took Sister Rachele to the administration building, to their superior who had come all the way from the capital Kampala when the news had reached the Comboni Headquarters. The parents followed them into the office, which soon became too small.

With difficulty Rachele related her story. But she was constantly overwhelmed by emotion and had to pause several times. Some parents bitterly reacted to the fact that their daughters had been left behind. Rachele felt wrought by guilt. Had they made the right decision? she wondered. Should they have faced the rebels instead of hiding?

'Of course, if the rebels had come to us first, we would have talked to them,' Sister Alba argued. 'But they didn't come to us. They went straight to the dormitories. It was clear that they wanted the girls. And there was no way we could have stopped them. They would have forced us to open the dormitories, all of them. If we had refused, they might have beaten us or even killed us. And we would have had no cause to follow them.'

She leaned towards Rachele and said emphatically: 'You have done what you could. You got back a hundred and nine. That is already a miracle.'

Suddenly, the news came that 30 girls were on their way. Sister Rachele jumped up, her face cleared up.

'Alba, did you hear that? Kony has sent a message to set them free. Our girls are coming home!' And before Alba could say anything she was gone. With some teachers she had climbed onto the trailer and left the campus.

Dusk had fallen when the group returned to the school, exhausted and utterly disappointed. They had searched the entire area. But it proved to be a false alarm. There was no trace of the girls.

6

The slain also shall be cast out, and their stink shall come up out of their carcasses, and the mountains shall be melted with their blood. (Isaiah 34,3)

The sun was low and the trees cast long shadows on the path. 'Where are they taking us?' Ellen wondered. They had been marching all day. She felt exhausted. Her feet and legs were full of scratches from the thorn bushes and the tall grass. Bad luck that she had lost her slippers. It happened during that ambush in the morning. They had just left their camp-site when the battle erupted. The attack took the rebels completely by surprise. In no time, however, they had taken up fighting positions and were putting up a fierce resistance. Ellen and her friends were herded under a big mango tree by their female guards. They had been sitting there for hours, listening to the rattling of guns, the explosions of bombs and once in a while the icy scream of someone who got hit.

A constant stream of wounded fighters was carried to their place under the mango tree. Their escorts then sat about making stretchers: gunny sacks tied to branches on which the wounded were laid without any first aid. Judging from the high number of casualties, Ellen had figured out that the rebels were on the losing end. In fact, she had been secretly hoping that they would be defeated and that the army would come and rescue them. But then heavy mortar fire had cleaved the air, followed by a loud scream, and suddenly a deadly silence had descended upon the battlefield. Not long afterwards, the commander had emerged, his swollen lip trembling, and he had ordered them to move. They hastily left, without even burying their dead.

Her group commander, Ojara, too must have died in that battle, Ellen realised. She hadn't seen him since. She looked at the endless plains that stretched in front of her, each step taking her further away from home. The sun sank glowing red behind the cassava fields. With night falling, a cool breeze got up. Still they kept on marching. At break-neck speed they were marched around Gulu district. Ellen gradually got the feeling that there was no final destination, that they were moving in circles and that the walking was an end in itself. Maybe that was the rebels' tactic: to keep on moving, so as to distract the army.

She glanced at the distorted faces of the wounded that were carried along on makeshift stretchers. Some were in a real bad state. Most were her age and even younger.

It was completely dark when the column finally came to a stand-still. Lagira ordered his juniors to set up camp. Ellen dropped down. Her head was spinning and her feet had become all numb. She scanned the place, which the rebels called Te-Atoo. It was probably another one of their secret camp-sites. When she saw the wounded being carried into a thatched hut, she guessed this must be the sick-bay.

Without any explanation, Ellen and her four schoolmates who had been assigned to Ojara's group were transferred to another unit. Their new commander was called Owino, a short, slim man in his early 20s. Even before they could recover, he ordered them to prepare food.

'If you refuse to work, you'll get a bullet,' he snorted. 'Or shall I teach you how to serve a man?'

While Ellen was preparing the fire, he talked non-stop. He had been abducted eight years ago and had grown up as Kony's escort, he said. After all those years, he had adapted and accepted Kony's activities. Therefore, he had been promoted to second lieutenant.

'In the end you too will submit to the will of the Lord's Resistance Army', he predicted. 'There is no other way.' He pointed at his wife. 'Look at Ajok. Once she was cut off from the rest of us during a battle. She had the chance of a lifetime to escape. But she didn't. She followed our trail and came back. You know why?' He paused to look at them. Then he burst into laughter. 'Because she couldn't leave me!'

Ellen felt nothing but disgust for that man. She tried to concentrate on the fire, taking care that it did not give off smoke. If it did, they would be beaten, the commander had warned.

Owino went on boasting about his bravery on the battlefield. 'We recently killed a doctor near Otwal because he refused to lead us to the next army position. A famous doctor!' The stories made her shiver. Was this what Kony was doing to the abducted children? Turning them into killing machines, monsters who mercilessly killed their own people? Was this what Owino meant by 'adapting' and 'accepting Kony's activities'? She was determined to keep on resisting, whatever the price would be.

***

Norman stared gloomily into the night. He had just got the news that his group commander, Ojara, passed away. Ojara had been shot in the belly and he died on the way to the sick-bay. Norman had seen his badly wounded body, his stomach spilling out.

What a massacre! Five dead and many injured, all of them abducted children like himself. Fortunately, he had managed to get hold of the mortar ground plate. Otherwise, he might have been killed too. He knew how to operate that mortar launcher. After all, he was part of Support, the unit that specialised in bombs and mines. It was a matter of speed: firing two mortar bombs and then running away with the ground plate before the other side had the chance to fire back. He had no idea how many casualties the enemy had suffered, but the fact that they retreated shortly afterwards had led him to believe that there were many. How much longer could he take this? Norman wondered. How much longer would he be lucky and come out alive? It was like a cruel gamble: entering the battlefield, always walking straight while firing ahead, hoping and praying that the enemy's bullets would not hit him. The rules were engraved in his head. They were not allowed to lie down or look for cover in a battle. Those who ran away or showed signs of fear would be killed, but those who stood and fought would be protected. The commanders, who mostly stayed behind, saw to it that everyone followed the rules. Those who disobeyed were punished, sometimes even shot by their own commanders. The enemy lurked on both sides and Norman didn't know whom to fear most.

He glanced at the Aboke girls who were preparing the meal. For a boy like him, it was forbidden to talk to them. He was only allowed to pass on the orders of the commanders. They didn't know yet what lay ahead of them, he thought bitterly. They didn't know what plans Kony had in store for them. The thought of his own participation in their sorry fate made him even more depressed.

How to get out of this mess? It was too risky to even think about escaping. And where would he run to? The army would skin him alive. He had attacked so many of their barracks and crippled their soldiers with his mines. No, he had to forget about escaping. After all, Kony was going to overthrow the government by the first of January, as the Holy Spirit had predicted. Several earlier deadlines had already passed but this time it seemed serious. They were winning one battle after another. Kony would then become the president of Uganda and come looking for him.

There was yet another thought that deterred him. If he escaped, the rebels might attack his homestead and take revenge on his family. He had seen it happen before. Only a month ago, a boy from Awach had run away with his gun. Together with the students abducted from Sir Samuel Baker School, Norman had been sent to the culprit's homestead to avenge his escape. The inhabitants, including the boy's parents, had been rounded up, their arms tied behind their backs and made to lie down. Then the boys of Samuel Baker were ordered to smash their heads with poles from the granary. Before leaving, they had destroyed the entire homestead, felling the mango trees and setting fire to the huts.

Norman took a deep breath. Was there no escape then? Was he to spend the rest of his life in this madness, until his body, like that of the others, was left on the battlefield, riddled with bullets, prey to the vultures?

He got up and went for supper.

7

*But they rebelled, and vexed his holy spirit: therefore he was
turned to be their enemy. (Isaiah 63, 10)*

The 25-mile road from Kampala to Entebbe International Airport was
bustling with activity. Dusk was falling. Clouds of smoke from charcoal
stoves hovered like mysterious ghosts over the hills and valleys of the
Ugandan capital. They covered the crowds sitting in the bars and
restaurants along the road or hauling bunches of bananas and bags of
maize. Sister Rachele took in the scenes with a special interest. It was
as if she saw Kampala for the first time. The sprawling markets, the
laughing faces, the packed buses: this was the other Uganda. The
Uganda that prospered and boomed. The Uganda that had known peace
and development for the last ten years. The Uganda the world knew
best.

What a difference with the north. The Nile drew a natural border
between the two regions. When one crossed Karuma bridge from the
south, a different world emerged, a world of destruction and terror
and paralysing fear. Sister Rachele could vividly remember how the
war in the north began. The soldiers of Obote's and Okello's armies
fled home after they had been defeated in the middle of the eighties.
Still armed, they caused great insecurity in the northern region. The
new government of Museveni didn't have enough troops to control
the entire area. In Aboke, there was only one patrol unit. Once it had
left, the school fell prey again to looting soldiers. When Museveni
finally took the north, the Acholi soldiers crossed into Sudan, where
they regrouped and resumed the war. They feared reprisals for earlier
massacres, particularly in the Luwero Triangle. With their propaganda
they caused large parts of the population to follow them. Alice Lakwena
had been a crucial factor in uniting and organising the resistance against
the new regime. When her army was defeated, most former soldiers
accepted Museveni's offer of amnesty and put down their arms,

spurring on the majority of the refugees to return home. But a hard core continued fighting.

The war had been dragging on ever since. Sometimes, it was quiet for months, prompting everyone to believe that Kony's resistance had died out like a candle light. But then, unexpectedly, the rebels invaded again from Sudan, better trained and equipped than ever before. Roads and schools closed down, communication ceased and the area retreated into splendid isolation.

In fact, the rebels' activities had mainly been confined to the districts of Gulu and Kitgum, the heartland of the Acholi, Sister Rachele realised. Apac, where her school was located, had largely been spared. Sporadically, there had been rumours of abductions in the area. The school then prayed for peace and reconciliation. But only now, she thought with a sense of shame, only now that her own girls had been kidnapped, was she speaking out, was she actually doing something about the plight of the abducted children.

She closed her eyes. Maybe this was her mission: to be part of this suffering, to bring these abuses into the open in the hope that one day her girls and all the other children would be free. Never before had an abduction in Uganda received so much attention. Even the international media had reported it. After all, it was the first case that was so clear and irrefutable. The rebels had tried to deny it. Not they but the Ugandan army had taken the Aboke girls, their spokesman in the Kenyan capital Nairobi claimed. Rachele had been shocked by this blatant lie. Fortunately, she had a hundred and ten witnesses!

And here she was on her way to Nairobi to try and meet that spokesman. At the expense of the Ugandan government too. She took a deep breath. A lot had happened in the past week. They had continued to search the area for two days, moving even up to the place where she had left the girls. She found out that the rebels had stayed the night there, and that a fierce battle had taken place the next morning. Eight government soldiers had reportedly been killed in that battle, and two abducted boys had managed to escape. From the boys they learnt that the group had been heading for Atoo hill. But however much she had begged people to take her there, nobody thought a new meeting possible or advisable. In the end, she had turned to the highest military authorities in Gulu for help. She had put three questions to the commander. How could she reach the rebels again? Could she speak to the President of Uganda? And what could he do to rescue the girls?

The commander had introduced her to General Salim Saleh, the president's brother and the adviser on military and political affairs for the north. The general had already heard about her pursuit. His colonel had even spotted her from the helicopter when she was moving with the rebels. 'Help me to reach Lagira again, she had begged him. I'm sure I can talk to that man.' But he had looked at her in disbelief. 'Believe me, sister, they are already sorry that they gave you those one hundred and nine.'

Then he had picked up the phone. 'Do you want to talk to the president?' A few minutes later she was talking to President Museveni in person. She briefly told him what had happened. When she finished, there was a long pause at the other end.

'I'm coming to Gulu,' Museveni then said. 'I'm coming for the children.' His wife, Janet, too came on the phone and together they had said a prayer for the remaining girls.

With a feeling of gratitude Sister Rachele recalled her meeting with the president at the military headquarters in Gulu two days later. There were only the two of them. She told him everything. She even mentioned the fact that the soldiers had let them down at that crucial moment. 'I have to find a way to get to Kony,' she had said at the end. 'Maybe through his spokesman in Nairobi. I also would like to meet the President of Sudan. There are rumours that our children are being taken to Sudan.'

Museveni had been pondering for a while. Then he had called his secretary. 'We are going to organise a trip to Nairobi for the sister', he had said. 'But she is not going alone. She will take one of her sisters along.' Then he had spelled out his plan. He would organise for her to meet the head of the International Committee of the Red Cross in Nairobi. That man could possibly help her to get to Kony's spokesman. But before leaving, she first had to meet the Libyan ambassador in Kampala. That too he would arrange for her. 'We have no direct relations with the government of Sudan', he had explained. 'The Libyan envoy is our go-between. That man can help you to meet the Sudanese ambassador in Nairobi.'

She took another breath as she looked at the airport looming in the distance. There was so much she didn't understand. There were so many actors involved whose motives she didn't know. But maybe she didn't need to know them. She was not to play politics or to take sides. Her task was to campaign for the release of her girls and all the abducted children. For there was one thing she knew for sure: it was terribly wrong to involve children in war. Whatever reasons adults might have to fight, children should at all times be left out!

8

*And the destruction of the transgressors and of the sinners shall
be together, and they that forsake the Lord shall be consumed.
(Isaiah 1, 28)*

Ellen found it amazing how easily the human body adapted to new
and extremely harsh conditions. Even the long walking hours she had
grown used to. Her limbs and muscles were not aching as much in the
morning. And her feet had become as hard as shoe soles. She had been
with the rebels for over a week now and she had gradually settled into
the daily routine. Every morning before sunrise they were woken up
by the clapping of hands. Then they started marching, until sunset.
Sometimes, they stopped at noon for lunch, but never longer than for
two hours. Mostly, they walked all day long. The speed was very high.
They could cover up to 30 miles a day. Fortunately, Ellen did not have
to carry heavy loads like most of the other recruits. Some were hauling
crates of soda or bags of sugar of up to 50 kg.

At night they usually slept in the bush. When it rained, a piece of
plastic sheeting was tied to the trees and grass was heaped up on the
ground so that the water could not reach them. They only had a sheet
to cover themselves. The sweaters of their friends proved to be very
useful in the cold morning hours. They were wearing their school
uniforms day and night. They looked pretty filthy by now. Thanks to
Sarah, Ellen could change her shirt every other day. Her friend from
Senior Four had grabbed two shirts before leaving and they took turns
wearing the second one, while the first one was put out to dry.

On rare occasions like last night, they slept in a deserted homestead.
The inhabitants, Ellen knew, had fled to the town centres or to one of
the protected camps, located around an army post. Only some elder
people and pregnant women stayed behind. The rebel commanders
then interrogated them about the positions of the government troops
and forcibly took whatever food and water was available. When there

was nothing to eat, recruits were sent to the neighbouring fields and villages to loot. Ellen then saw them return with beans, cassava, chickens and goats. And once in a while, when they had attacked a trading centre, they also brought sugar and tea. But the Aboke girls were never involved in such raids. In a way they were privileged. They only had to collect water and cook food. For the rest, they were guarded day and night. Even when they were going to the toilet or fetching firewood, an escort was sent along.

Ellen had an additional advantage: she spoke Acholi, the language of the commanders. She often chatted with them to show that she was not afraid, that she actually liked them. That was her trick: to win the commanders' confidence so that they would become less alert and then she would get a chance to escape.

The wake-up sign was given. Ellen jumped up, wrapped up her sheet and grabbed her cooking utensils. They were ready to leave when Lagira discovered that one of the recruits was missing. His face turned grim, almost unrecognisable. 'If you don't find her, I will kill one of the Aboke girls!' he yelled. As if to prove his point, he made some Aboke girls lie down. Ellen stared at the scene with disbelief. This savage fury was something she had never seen in a man. She sensed something terrible was going to happen. Suddenly, a loud scream made her look up.

'Here she is!' The rebels pulled the missing girl out of one of the huts. Ellen knew her. She was a child from Aboke village, a few years younger than herself. The rebels beat her up and kicked her terribly. One of them jumped on her chest with his boots. The girl groaned and tried to worm her way out, her eyes pleading for help. But there was no escape. The blows rained down on her from everywhere. Then Lagira called the Aboke girls. 'Finish her off,' he ordered coldly. They were told to grab wooden logs and beat her. Ellen felt her legs trembling. She tried to do the trick again, transcend her body and let somebody else take over, but it didn't work anymore. Hesitantly, she followed her friends to collect firewood. Then they surrounded the girl and started hitting her lightly on the legs.

'Not like that!' one of the rebels screamed. He demonstrated how they should hit her hard on the neck and the back of the head. The girls cried and looked at each other and just kept quiet. Lagira became even more furious. He made them line up and beat the girl one by one. Those who didn't beat hard enough, were slapped and forced to repeat. Their victim was now bleeding heavily from the head. When the last one had passed, she seemed dead but was still shaking. One of the commanders came forward and hit her a last time, to make sure she was dead.

Then the rebels set upon the pregnant woman who had hidden her. She too was beaten up viciously, until she didn't move anymore. Lagira ordered everyone to start moving. Ellen felt sick. She no longer managed to look fearless and strong. There was only confusion and disgust. Disgust for Lagira and the rebels, but also for herself. She felt as if this act had cut her off forever from St Mary's and the world she came from. As if her life would never be the same again. She stared in the distance at the vast, rolling plains that stretched away to a horizon where sorrow was infinite. Why? she wondered. Why did Lagira behave like this? Why was he killing his own people? And why was he using children to do that?

At the next stop all the Aboke girls were summoned. Lagira's face was distorted with anger. He almost spat out the words as he accused them of having encouraged the girl to escape. 'You are stubborn and disobedient. You refuse to work. And you sit on chairs, as if you were men. Don't you know that girls are supposed to sit on the floor?' His eyes narrowed. 'Even if Kony decides to release you, I will not let you go. I will kill you and say that I let you go.'

Then he ordered his escorts to bring Acii. A wounded girl was taken in front of them. Her buttocks were so badly infected that she could hardly stand up. 'Acii here tried to escape,' Lagira said. 'But she was caught. This is what will happen to you too if you try to run away.' Then he ordered them to lie flat on their bellies. They would be punished with 50 strokes. Those who moved or cried would get a double beating. He changed his mind and settled for 15 strokes. Ellen felt the blows burning on her buttocks. She clenched her teeth in pain and managed not to stir or groan. But Palma and Sandra couldn't stand the pain. They had touched the painful spots in an attempt to protect themselves. So they got another round. Ellen and her friends had to watch while the two girls were beaten terribly, without looking away, without showing any emotions.

When Ellen returned to her position, tears rolled down her face. But on reaching her unit she quickly brushed them away. Her commander could betray her and she would be beaten again. Her buttocks were bleeding. It hurt to sit down. As she was fanning the fire, she again and again saw the begging eyes of the little girl. What an awful, senseless death! And she had taken part in her killing. Her hands had helped to beat that girl to death. She had never thought she would kill somebody in her life, let alone a child. They forced me, she kept telling herself. I could not do otherwise. They forced me!

Owino suddenly put his gumboot under her nose.

'Take off!'

She didn't move. She would teach them a lesson, she thought, seething with anger. So that they would realise they were wrong. She assembled all her courage and said without looking at him: 'I only do that for my father.'

He pushed the boot closer to her nose.

'Then from now on, you will treat me as your father.' She kept on fanning the flames. The strained silence made the others look up. 'Do it, Ellen,' they pleaded. 'Do it!' The boot was still there. The tension was getting unbearable. At last, she put down her plate and with visible contempt pulled off his boots, not once looking up at him.

9

And I will punish the world for their evil... Their children also
shall be dashed to pieces before their eyes; their houses shall
be spoiled, and their wives ravished. (Isaiah 13, 11-16)

It was boiling hot in the Kenyan capital Nairobi. A cloud of exhaust
fumes covered the long queues of people along Kenyatta Avenue. They
squeezed into one of the packed *matatu* buses which then edged their
way through the chaotic traffic, African music blaring from the open
windows.

Sister Rachele was glad she could flee the hustle and bustle of the
capital. In the hotel lobby, she wiped the sweat off her forehead. She
had been in Nairobi for almost three weeks now and she was missing
her school; she was missing Aboke. She felt painfully cut off from
events in northern Uganda. Of course, she would be informed
immediately if there was any news. But that was exactly what made
her so restless: that there was no news. The 30 girls seemed to have
disappeared from the earth.

For weeks, she had been searching the newspapers for the slightest
piece of information, but there was none on Lagira's unit. She did
read about another attack. Nineteen people were said to have been
killed when they fell into a rebel ambush near Murchison Falls. But
the attack was attributed to another group, led by Commander Lagony.
She had also learnt about President Museveni's new strategy in the
fight against the Lord's Resistance Army, the 'combined armed
elements'. All means would be used simultaneously to fight the rebels
and free the captives: helicopter gunships, armoured vehicles called
mambas, and fast-moving ground troops. The army claimed the strategy
was bearing fruit. According to their spokesman, 23 rebels had been
killed in recent weeks and 114 captives freed, again all from Lagony's
unit. The commander himself was said to be wounded. General Salim
Saleh had offered Shs 2.5 million for anyone who could give

information about Lagony's whereabouts. To Sister Rachele the news of the new strategy was worrying. Excessive force, she feared, would only endanger the children. Had she not seen how the captives were used as a human shield by the rebels?

Only once had the Aboke girls been mentioned in the media. In an unusually sharp condemnation, Pope John Paul II had called for their immediate release. 'This Sunday of missionary prayers is blighted by the news of the abduction of a group of students of the Catholic school of Aboke in the north of Uganda,' he said in the *Post Angelus* of 20 October 1996. 'Thirty girls are now in the hands of their abductors, while their families and the Catholic community are in anguish over their fate. I appeal to the conscience of those responsible to bring this brutal kidnapping to an end: respect the lives and dignity of these young people! In the name of God, I ask for their immediate liberation.'

And here she was with her superior in this huge, strange city and she felt she was not getting anywhere. Everyone had been very helpful though. The Ugandan high commissioner in Nairobi was constantly up and about, making appointments, consulting Kampala and making sure they had a car and a driver at their disposal. Shortly after their arrival, he had taken them to the office of the International Committee of the Red Cross. They were received by Goeff, the regional director. The Irishman had taken a lot of time to listen to her story. He was more than willing to help. But when Sister Rachele formulated her request, his face had looked doubtful. It would not be easy to talk to Kony's spokesman, he had predicted. The man had to agree to meet her. He suggested that any communication should pass through him, and be conducted in utmost secrecy. Sister Rachele didn't even know to whom Geoff was talking.

It was a time-consuming and frustrating process. Every question was returned by another question. And the answer took days. First, her invisible interlocutors claimed they knew nothing of the Aboke girls. Then she was asked to give a detailed description of the commander she had met. She replied that he had introduced himself as Mariano Ocaya and that he had a swollen upper lip. A few days later came another message: yes, they recognised him as one of their leaders but they didn't know if he had the girls. Again she had to provide additional information. The last message said: 'We cannot do anything from Nairobi. We have to contact the field. If we have the girls, they must be in the field. And the field is in Uganda.'

'I have to talk to these people directly. Ask if they can receive me,' she had begged Geoff. But the answer was negative. 'They don't want to meet you.' He had gently urged her to go back to Uganda. This could go on for weeks. He promised to keep her informed of any further developments through the Comboni Mission head office in Kampala. If there was a breakthrough, he would personally come over to Uganda.

The second part of their mission had been equally disappointing. They did manage to see the Sudanese ambassador. His Libyan colleague had kept his word and they were received a few days after their arrival. The ambassador too had listened with great interest to what Sister Rachele had to say. In the end she had handed him a list with the names of the girls. 'Our fear is that the children will be taken to Sudan,' she had explained.

He had studied the list. Then he stood up, pointing at a map on the wall. 'Our first garrison across the border is Kajo Keji. I will ask our army unit there to be on the lookout for the girls. If they arrive there, our soldiers should immediately inform the headquarters in Juba and arrange to send them back.' He would also inform his government and promised to get back to her as soon as he had any information. The meeting had given her new hope. She felt she had done something useful, she had spoken to somebody who could actually do something. But afterwards she never heard from the man again.

Promises, always promises. But then, what else could she do but keep on hoping, keep on trying? She owed it to the 30 girls she had been forced to leave behind. She owed it to the parents who lived in cruel uncertainty. She owed it to herself too: it was the only way to continue living after the abduction. She swore she would not rest until all the girls were back. Even if she had to give her life for it.

Her attention was caught by an article faxed to her from Uganda. It was an interview with a student of Sir Samuel Baker School who had escaped from Lagira's unit. The group was on its way to meet the wounded Commander Lagony, the boy was quoted as saying. Lagony was supposed to come and pick up the Aboke girls and bring them to Sudan, after Lagira had failed three times to cross the border. One paragraph in particular struck her. 'The school girls are being treated in a special manner because they are brown skinned and tall Langi girls as ordered by Kony. The girls are constantly anointed with shea nut oil.'

Sister Rachele closed her eyes. A lot was becoming clear now. At the same time, she realised this was bad news. It meant that the girls were indeed on their way to Sudan. Getting them back from there would be difficult, if not impossible. It also meant that the chances of releasing them were slim: Kony himself had ordered their abduction. Her mind was suddenly made up. She would go back to Uganda, to the field. There was not much more she could do here.

10

Their cities are destroyed, so that there is no man that there is none inhabitant. (Zephaniah 3, 6)

Ellen could no longer make sense of it. She tried in vain to find a pattern, a purpose in all this moving up and down, splitting into smaller units and then coming together again. But either there was no pattern and their only purpose was to scare away the population, clear the land of its people. Or, they were going somewhere but for some reason were unable to reach that destination. She sensed that a lot was happening in the outside world: events which the commanders could follow over the radio but which were kept hidden from them. For hours a day, they were sitting near their transmitters. Sometimes they used another language, which she thought was Arabic.

Very little from the outside world got through to them, the recruits. They were totally emerged in the world of the Lord's Resistance Army, a world with its own laws and rules and obscure logic. A world where one didn't ask questions or show feelings, where one simply obeyed and executed orders. Everything they had learned at St Mary's was turned upside down here. Killing was good, refusing to kill was bad. Cruelty was good, mercy was bad.

In that savage world Joseph Kony seemed to be the absolute ruler. The rebels called him their father and believed that the Holy Spirit, which they called *Lakwena*, told him what to do. 'Lakwena said we should do this,' the rebels then passed on his orders. Or: 'Lakwena said we should not do that'. At times they were told not to cook with oil from the *yaa* tree. Lakwena had said so. At other times the commanders had to refrain from sex. Lakwena had said so. When it started raining, they were ordered to let the water run on their faces for four minutes. Orders from Lakwena. Women who were on 'O.P.' were not allowed to cook or share a meal with other rebels. And time and again, they were told that they were about to overthrow the government. Lakwena had said so.

Ellen had heard that name before. There was the witch, Alice Lakwena. As far as the legend went, Alice disappeared in the waters of the Nile for 40 days and re-emerged as a prophetess, claiming she could cure people of all kinds of illnesses. Many people truly believed she had magical powers. After Museveni came to power, she joined the Acholi rebellion and commanded her own unit. But when her army was defeated, she fled to neighbouring Kenya, where, as far as Ellen knew, she was still living in a refugee camp.

In many ways, Kony's cult was a copy of Alice Lakwena's. Some rituals reminded Ellen of the stories she had heard at the time. Such as the egg ritual, which was performed two weeks after their abduction. A big circle had been drawn in the sand, divided into 30 squares. The Aboke girls were told to bathe. Then they had to stand bare chested in the squares. Lagira stood in the middle, holding a raw egg in his hand. He dipped the egg in a brew of ashes and water and then drew the picture of a heart on their chests and backs, and a cross on their foreheads, shoulders and hands. This was their camouflage, he told them. It would protect them from the bullets. If the egg broke, the person was possessed with evil spirits and had to be killed. 'What we are doing is written in the Bible.' Ellen had held her breath. Since the killing of that girl, she knew he was capable of anything. But to everyone's relief, the egg had passed the circle without breaking.

For the next three days, they were not allowed to bathe or dress, so as not to erase the symbols. If the heart and crosses were wiped out, it would be seen as a sign that they were thinking of escaping. Ellen's heart on the back was gone after only one day, from carrying her cooking pot. 'Luckily we don't have to worry about you,' Owino had laughed. 'You are already so used to us that you would be the last one to escape.' Since the day she had refused to pull off his boots, she had felt a change in the commanders' behaviour towards her. As if she had earned their respect. Her trick was working. She only had to keep on pretending.

In reality, she tried to keep her head cool and find out what was really happening out there. Only once did news from the outside world reach them. That was when the pope called for the release of the Aboke girls. The broadcast on Radio Uganda had enraged the commanders. Lagira had summoned them immediately. 'Who do you think you are?' he had yelled. 'The pope didn't intervene for any of the other children. What is so special about you?' He had waved his finger at them. 'The government accuses us. Other countries accuse us. Because of you everybody is now against us. From now on you are soldiers of the movement. I will never let you go. Never!'

Ellen looked around the camp, which was now very crowded. There were hundreds of rebels, three units altogether. First they had met the group of Lagony. She had heard that name mentioned before. Like Lagira, Lagony was a notorious commander. And like Lagira, he was said to be cruel. But she didn't get to see him. He was carried to the sick-bay straight away, reportedly with a bullet in his thigh. His subordinate, Commander Otim, had taken over the command of his unit. The Aboke girls had been split up: one group had stayed with Lagira, while Ellen and 14 other girls had left with Otim. For one week, they roamed around the villages and fields of Gulu, while the rebels constantly brought in loot, before they linked up with the others again. Ellen had been delighted to see that all her schoolmates were still alright. Except for Justine, who was wounded in the neck. It had not been easy to find out what had happened. Only on the way to collecting water were they able to exchange some information. In that way, Ellen learnt that Lagira's group had run into an ambush of the government troops, in which the rebels suffered great losses. A bullet had glanced off Justine's throat. She also learnt that Pamela burnt herself while cooking.

And then, last night, a third unit joined them, led by a certain Commander Omona. The meeting took place at the other side of Aswa river. Crossing the river had been scary. There was no bridge so they had to hoist themselves across on a rope. Like most children in Uganda, Ellen could not swim. Mainly because they did not have much to carry, she and her schoolmates made it safely to the other bank. But those carrying heavy loads could not hold on to the rope. Eight children fell down and were swept away by the current. Nobody seemed to care.

The meeting with commander Omona had been particularly unpleasant. He was a man in his 40s. From the first moment, Ellen had felt his eyes fixed on her. There was a strange glow in his look, which made her feel uneasy. Omona had taken the overall command of the three units. He was going to address them in the morning. But he had hardly started speaking when bombs rained down on them, forcing everyone to flee. For most of the day, they had been running, the government troops hot on their heels, before settling this new camp site.

Night was falling. For the second time, they were lined up, waiting for Omona's address. But the commanders seemed to be too busy discussing their future strategy. At last, Omona came over, only to inform them that they were going to cross the road to Kitgum the following morning. Ellen got a shock. Crossing the main road was a risky undertaking, she knew. They would have to leave the protection of the bush, which would make the chance of being spotted much higher. Moreover, the main road was patrolled by soldiers and 'local defence' units: civilians who had voluntarily subscribed to defend their villages.

Omona was selecting the front troops, rebels who were told to go and take up positions so as to 'open up' the road in the early morning hours. The Aboke girls were dispersed. As Ellen walked back to her unit, she suddenly stood still, staring with wide open eyes at the line of soldiers who were leaving for the road. That was him, she realised. That was her half brother. He had been abducted a year ago and they had never heard from him again. He recognised her too and stopped, staring silently. She knew this was a dangerous moment. If they showed any recognition, they could be beaten up or even killed. They slowly crossed, looking at each other without speaking, with tears welling up in their eyes.

The reunion with her brother had thrown Ellen into utter confusion. She couldn't get rid of his image for the rest of the night. For hours she was lying awake, thinking of him. She felt excited that he was still alive and that he was here with her in the camp. In a way, it made her feel less lonely. But there was another feeling, much deeper and intangible, which made her restless: the thought that in one year, she too might still be with the rebels. That maybe she would have to spend the rest of her life with them in the bush. She tried to shake off the depressing thoughts. Surely, the sister would do everything possible to get them released. Or she would escape. No, she could never give up the hope of getting free.

The next morning the atmosphere was tense. The commanders were nervously pacing up and down. Everybody was ordered to take their positions. In long parallel lines, they hid in the tall grass by the side of the road. Ellen and her schoolmates were up in front, their escorts behind them. She scanned the other rebels, hoping to catch another glimpse of her half-brother. But there was no sign of him.

For more than two hours they waited at the side of the road. When finally the whistle was blown, Ellen jumped up and ran as fast as she could to the other side. Behind her all hell broke loose. Machine guns were rattling, bullets whistling in the air and rocket grenades exploding. Even from the air they were under fire. In blind terror, Ellen ran through the elephant grass. She felt her heart pounding and her ears singing. It was now a matter of survival, of keeping on running, away from the rattling and whistling. When the worst noise had died away, she risked a look back. Her escorts were running behind her. There was no way to find out if her friends had made it.

It took until nightfall before a full assessment could be made. There were lots of casualties. Even Oyet had been hit. Ellen could find no more trace of her brother. He had disappeared as suddenly as he had come. The thought that he might have been killed deeply upset her. Then she counted her schoolmates. Twenty eight, twenty nine. Her breath stopped short and she counted again. Twenty nine. Somebody was missing. The news spread like fire. Eva was not there. Did she escape? Nobody even dared pronounce the word. Fortunately, the commanders were too busy tending the wounded to take much notice. 'Maybe she got killed or wounded,' one of them shrugged.

That evening they were split up again. Ellen moved to a new unit, where she was the only Aboke girl. She was assigned to the 'family' of the radio man, Anywar, and his two wives. Fifteen Aboke girls left the same evening with Lagira. The wounded were carried along on stretchers. Ellen watched the line being swallowed by the darkness.

Sarah, her friend with whom she had shared the second shirt, was among them. She had the unsettling feeling that this time they were separated for good, that she might not see her friend again.

***

Sister Rachele looked around the table with obvious satisfaction. Her face had cleared up and she was even able to laugh, which made her look ten years younger. They were seated in the dining room of the military headquarters in Gulu. Opposite her was President Museveni and next to her, shifting shyly and uneasily, sat Eva. Rachele had been overwhelmed with joy when news reached her that Eva had escaped. She had immediately set off for Gulu, a two-hour drive from Aboke. But seeing Eva had been a shock. The girl was in a terrible state. Her feet and legs were swollen and in her eyes was a profound sadness. This was not the innocent look of a teenager. This was the weary look of a woman who had seen things too terrible for words.

'Sister, when the pope spoke, we were beaten,' was the only thing she said when Rachele embraced her. Then she retreated again into her silent world. The president, who happened to be in Gulu to inspect his troops, had promptly invited them to lunch. And here they were, the three of them. Museveni looked clearly pleased with Eva's escape. He asked her all kinds of questions about life in the bush and the rebels' movements and tactics. Eva gradually started to relax a bit. She told them about the girl they were forced to kill, about the pursuits by the army and the constant fighting. She explained how during these battles, the captives had to sit in the middle, while the rebels around them put up resistance.

Sister Rachele took advantage of Eva's opening up.

'And the other girls, how are they doing?'

'They are all still alive. Justine got hit in the neck and Palma burned herself while cooking.'

'Are they all in Uganda?'

'They are, but the rebels were preparing to leave for Sudan.'

The president glanced at Sister Rachele. His face looked grave.

'Sister, we should get all of them released. And I don't mean only the Aboke girls. There are thousands of children in Kony's hands. We have to think of them as well.'

Sister Rachele bent forward, fixing her brown eyes on the president.

'Allow me, Your Excellency, but why don't you stop this war? Our people have suffered enough. Let us finally have peace. Please, talk to those people.' He considered her suggestion for a while. 'OK,' he then said. 'I think I can leave both ways open: the military road and the road of peace. And we will see which one works.'

She shook her head. 'The military road will not lead anywhere, Your Excellency.'

11

Therefore deliver up their children to the famine, and pour out their blood by force of the sword; and let their wives be bereaved of their children and be widows; and let their men be put to death; let their young men be slain by the sword in battle. (Jeremiah 18, 21)

Failed attempt, Sarah cursed in silence as she walked behind Lagira. Crossing the main road had been her chance in a lifetime to escape. Eva had made it. Why hadn't she? She fought back tears of disappointment. They had prepared it well, though. The moment the firing started, the four of them would run in the opposite direction. In order to run faster, she had even thrown away the plastic sheeting. But maybe their group had been too large: they had simply been herded back by the guards. Fortunately, nobody had realised that they were trying to escape. They had a good excuse; they were only fleeing from the fighting.

Life in the bush had been extremely hard for 15-year-old Sarah. She was not so talkative and outgoing as her friend Ellen. Most of the time she was quiet and withdrawn. In the five weeks since their abduction, she had hardly talked to anyone. She didn't speak Acholi well anyway. She came from Soroti in eastern Uganda and belonged to a tribe that was different from the northern people. Kony's war seemed utterly senseless to her, and the rebels the most cruel creatures she had ever come across. Those who had been with the rebels for five or six years were the worst. She felt nothing but aversion towards those grubby, filthy-looking boys with their long, uncombed hair and ragged clothes. They had grown up in the Lord's Resistance Movement. Some could hardly remember their relatives and had never seen the inside of a classroom. Violence had become like a game to them. The eagerness with which they killed and tortured shocked her. They even competed with each other in brutality and were encouraged to compete by the commanders. The more they abducted and looted and killed, the higher they climbed in rank.

Though Sarah kept very much to herself, she carefully registered everything around her. By making herself almost invisible, she could observe her surroundings more easily. She felt this was the thing she had to do: observing, storing it all away, for later, for the day she would be free. Though she wondered if she would find the right words for the scenes that were stuck in her mind. Such as the incident with the cyclist. It was just before they were reunited with Ellen's group when the rebels spotted a man riding down the path. He tried to get away but the rebels had already grabbed him. 'Why do you ride a bicycle?' Lagira questioned him. Didn't he know Kony's law banning the riding of bicycles? The man pointed at his leg, which was swollen and smeared with some local medicine. He couldn't walk and was on his way to the hospital for treatment, he stammered, and he pleaded for mercy. But Lagira coldly told him that his leg would be cut off, according to the rules. At that moment, a woman accidently bumped into them. She too was grabbed by the rebels. Lagira ordered her to kneel down and bite off the leg. If she refused to do so, she would be killed. With horror, Sarah witnessed how the woman did as she was told. But of course, she could not get through the bone, so Lagira gave her an axe. Even then, it took all her strength to cut the leg in two. Both were left behind on the road, crying.

Sarah wiped the sweat off her forehead. Her head was spinning and her muscles were aching. For a few days she had been plagued by violent fits of fever, making her alternately shiver with cold and break out in a sweat. There was nobody who looked after her or gave her any medication. She was relieved when, at last, the sun sank and the commander called it a day. The escort who always carried the mortars ordered them to make tea for Lagira. She had seen that boy before. He was very small and had the expression of a real rebel, but he never beat them or behaved cruelly. As she was collecting firewood, she heard loud voices at the officers' quarters. Shortly afterwards the Aboke girls were summoned. Lagira stood in front of them, scrutinising them one by one.

'Did Officer Peter Obwoya rape any of you after the abduction?' he inquired.

They all stared down, not replying.

'Why didn't you report him?'

Silence again.

'Did anybody else try to touch you?'

Some girls hesitantly came forward with the names of soldiers who had tried to 'corner' them. Lagira nodded with a grim look on his face and dismissed them. The next morning the punishments were distributed. Officer Peter Obwoya got 200 strokes for violating article nine: 'No fighter shall desire a woman or property which doesn't belong to him'. It was up to Kony to decide on further action to be taken, Lagira said. The others received 150 strokes each. Everbody had to watch as the soldiers were viciously beaten. Not much later Kony's verdict came by radio: 'elimination from the movement.' Without much ado the officer was tied and led away by Oyet and four rebels. 'I don't want to hear any gunshots,' Lagira ordered them. They disappeared into the jungle, bayonets fixed to their guns. Sarah thought it strange. All the commanders had one or more wives, most of them abducted girls. There must be a system by which a girl was assigned to a certain man, she gathered. Where and when this happened and who decided it, she couldn't figure out.

The journey continued unabated. Lagira had now personally taken responsibility for guarding the 15 Aboke girls. Sarah was glad her fever had subsided and she could think more clearly again. She noticed the everyday routine had changed. There was more looting than before. The rebels constantly brought in goats and chickens from the villages. More children were abducted too, as well as adults to carry the loot. 'We are going to Kampala,' Lagira said. But Sarah didn't believe him. The land around them was getting drier and hotter while Kampala, she knew, was lush and fertile. Besides, from the position of the sun she figured out they were heading northwards.

They stopped in the middle of the afternoon. Something seemed to be wrong. Then the rumour passed along the line: two newly abducted children had tried to escape. At the next stop, they were all assembled.

Sarah held her breath. She already knew what was to come. Lagira displayed that look again which spelled doom.

'I will once and for all teach you a lesson,' he lashed out. 'Because you helped those boys escape!' The recruits who were less than five months in the movement were told to lie down. Then the beating and kicking started. Sarah had already learnt how to avoid the blows. But for the newcomers it was the first time. Suddenly, she realised there was a pattern in the violence. It was not as arbitrary as it seemed. Each time new children were abducted, they were drilled like this, to break their resistance and deter them from escaping. Of course, if all the children escaped, there would not be much left of the Lord's Resistance Army, Sarah realised. As far as she could make out, the majority of the rebels were abducted children.

After the thrashing, they were taken to a small patch in the woods where the two boys were lying on the ground, their arms tied behind their backs. They looked not older than twelve. Nobody was allowed to look away while the rebels smashed their heads with an axe and speared them with bayonets. They even made jokes. 'Look how this one is crying for his mother!' And they all had to laugh. Then the axe was passed to the newcomers, who had to finish them off. Those who refused were beaten. 'Maybe you were also involved in the plan to escape,' the rebels shouted. When the boys had lost consciousness, the commander gave his bayonet to one of the newcomers.

'Check if they are still alive.'

The boy looked around helplessly.

'Pierce the heart!' the officer yelled.

It was a disgusting scene. One of the victims was still twitching and they gave him a final blow with the axe.

That evening it started raining. 'Where is the plastic sheeting?' Sarah heard Oyet ask. One of the guards pointed in her direction. Oyet came marching towards her, his eyes flickering.

'Go and lie down,' he ordered.

She went flat on her belly. He can't do anything, she told herself. Had Kony not sent a message that the Aboke girls should be kept alive? Oyet ordered one of the rebels to shoot her. For a split second, she panicked as she heard the rebel take position above her, load the gun and pull the trigger. But nothing happened and she was made to stand up again.

'If you lose something again, even a needle, I will kill you!' Oyet screamed, leaving her behind, trembling.

***

Norman was on guard. It was a task he didn't really mind. At least he didn't need to participate in the massacres. He would never get used to it, he thought. More than 50 children had been killed before his eyes, 'to teach them a lesson'. Small, nameless victims on the altar of Joseph Kony. Some had to stare into the barrel of a gun, their arms tied, but most were not so lucky as to be killed by a bullet. They were beaten, stoned or stabbed to death. And the newcomers had to take part in those killlings. Once in a while, somebody refused and was beaten or even killed. But most did not refuse: they were too terrified.

His own escape plan was gradually taking shape. It was the only thing he could think of. He was sick and tired of this life in the bush, of all the looting and fighting and killing. In the past days, they had been killing villagers only for crossing their path. 'Who told you to walk on the road?' Lagira then asked. 'You, Acholi, don't want to listen. When you're dead, you will understand better!' And he had ordered his rebels to finish them off with axes and bayonets.

Especially since the death of his friend, Oboya, there was no point in continuing this life. Oboya had been with the rebels for five years. He had taught Norman all the techniques to survive in the bush. In countless battles they had fought side by side. They had helped each other and warned one another when danger was looming. But when they crossed the road to Kitgum, Oboya was hit in the knee. He was carried to the sick-bay, but his groaning had alerted the army. The sick-bay got hit. Later Norman had stared at the dead body of his friend. Oboya was only 15.

Tears of grief welled up in his eyes. Now he was all alone, at the mercy of Lamola, his new commander since Ojara died. Oh, how he hated that man! Lamola was younger and smaller than him. Maybe that's why he mistreated him. He made Norman carry heavy loads. Apart from his gun and ammunition, Norman now also had to haul the mortars and the ground plate. If he dropped something or didn't move fast enough, he was beaten. He was even made to wash Lamola's clothes, as if he were his slave!

The whistle was blown. Norman hurried back to his unit. When he reached the group, he noticed that everybody had been split up again. He was to leave the same night with some of the captives. The Aboke girls were to stay behind with Lagira. They would cross the border later. Too late, he cursed himself as the line set itself in motion. As he moved towards Sudan, he knew that he would not see his country again for months. And that, for the third time, he would spend the turn of the year with the rebels.

***

Sarah was close to exhaustion. Her feet were torn. She had wrapped them with banana leaves in an attempt to ease the pain. They had been walking almost day and night for four days. There was hardly anything to eat or to drink. She felt weaker by the day. She could not give up, she kept telling herself. She had to force herself to put one foot after the other and try to close the gap between her and her predecessor. Giving up, she knew, meant certain death. Did she not hear the gunshots behind her, or the screaming of those who were being beaten to death? 'Do you want to rest?' Lagira asked every time somebody lagged behind or stumbled. If they said yes, he beat them to death with the simple words: 'Then you can rest forever!'

Others collapsed from hunger and dehydration; those who carried the heaviest loads fell first. Suddenly, there was no more distinction between the rebels and the recruits. They were all equal on this survival journey, in which nature made its inexorable selection. Only Lagira held out. He pushed the Aboke girls in front of him and seemed to become more brutal as the journey continued.

All of a sudden the line stopped in front of a stream. Sarah wondered where they were. They had crossed River Aswa some time back. She could not figure out which river this one was. Like last time, a rope was tied across the water and they had to pull themselves across. Sarah assembled her last strength. 'If I let go of the rope, I'm dead,' she told herself, trying not to look at the water swirling beneath her. To her own astonishment, she suddenly felt the ground under her feet again. With dazed eyes, she watched those who were too weak drop down and drown. Rebecca, one of the Aboke girls, fell too. But contrary to the others, she was rescued. 'Because she had not screamed', was the explanation.

There was no time to rest. They were hurried on again. On and on the journey went, over deserted land and rocky mountains. The sun hit them hard on the head. Sarah felt as if her throat was being choked. Her jerrycan, that she had filled up at the stream, was now completely empty. As far as the eye could reach, not a drop of water could be seen. She felt she was going to collapse when suddenly a collection of huts emerged on the skyline. At first she thought she was dreaming. But as she stumbled on, she could clearly see people, men in long white clothes. Arabs! Now she was convinced they were in Sudan. The Arabs welcomed them in a language she did not understand. They allowed them to rest in their camp, to have a drink of water and even to cook their food. Sarah felt infinitely grateful. One of the rebels installed the solar panel and Lagira made radio contact with 'headquarters' to inform them about where they were. Not much later an army truck with Sudanese number plates arrived. The sick and wounded were loaded onto it and taken away. Sarah and the rest stayed behind.

By evening they were told to start moving again, deeper into Sudan. With astonishment Sarah looked at the scenery around her. In the dimming light it looked like a place made of sky only. There were no tarmac roads, no cars, no houses and no people. Only sandy earth and low thorn bushes. When night had fallen, they stopped and slept where they were. Sarah lay awake for some time, staring at the stars which seemed so close she had the feeling she could touch them. The same sky and yet so far from home. What was she doing in this strange country, she wondered. And where was this journey going to end?

She must have fallen asleep as she woke up with a start. Dawn was breaking. The commander told them to continue. After a few miles, Ugandan-style huts appeared in the distance. Small children were standing by the side of the road, singing and clapping and waving branches at them. They sang Acholi songs.

'Welcome to Aru!' the commanders saluted them as they reached the camp. The Aboke girls were separated from the rest of the captives and herded into one of the huts. Kony was away, one of the commanders explained. But he would come soon. They had to wait for him. At last, Sarah thought, he would give in to the sister's request and set them free. At last, the nightmare would be over. Anxiously and with great hope, she waited for Kony.

12

And they that are left of you shall pine away in the iniquity of your enemies' lands; and also in the iniquities of their fathers shall they pine away with them. (Leviticus 26, 39)

A depressed group of people had gathered that Saturday morning under the mango tree at St Mary's school. The visitors shifted nervously on their wooden benches, sleepess nights could be read from some of their faces. Like every Saturday, the parents of the missing girls met at the school. They had formed the 'Concerned Parents Association', which lobbied for the release of the Aboke girls and all abducted children.

The initiative was born in those first fearful hours when the parents were waiting at the school for news from Sister Rachele. Dr Otim, an agricultural researcher at Makerere University, suggested that influential people who could help in getting the children released be contacted. They had written to embassies, UN organisations, human rights groups, church leaders and the press.

Later, they decided to unite into an association to coordinate their activities and build a network of support for the parents. Ben Pere, a retired businessman whose two daughters were taken in the Aboke raid, was elected chairman, and Angelina Atyam, a midwife from Lira, vice-chairperson.

This was a revolutionary initiative for Uganda. In the past, parents of abducted children did not dare protest for fear of reprisals. Many remembered the story of the man who was mutilated by the rebels because he had reported the kidnapping of his children to the police. His leg was cut off and he was forced to sit in front of his hut, as a deterrent to other villagers. But the Aboke parents were not only peasants from the north. They came from all over the country. Some were influential and vocal middle class people. They would not be intimidated. And until they had their children back, they would not keep quiet.

As Sister Rachele was away in Gulu, Sister Alba and Sister Mathilde took charge. They were busy serving tea and biscuits and comforting the visitors as best they could. The meeting started with a prayer. 'God, may you reach the abductors so that you can use your powers to release the victims,' one of the parents said. Then Ben Pere gave a summary of the contacts and efforts made so far. They had published an open letter to Joseph Kony in the newspapers, thanking him for releasing the 109 students and requesting him to release the other 30. They had met President Museveni. They had contacted the local authorities and turned to the Red Cross for help. He could not go into details, Ben stressed, as publicity could derail these efforts and endanger the lives of the children.

Angelina read out some of the reactions that had come in. The French, Belgian and Italian ambassadors expressed sympathy and promised to take up the matter with their governments. The reaction of the British high commissioner was considered rather strange. What the north needed was development, the envoy said in a letter. 'What we need first and foremost is our children!' Angelina exclaimed. 'And peace! How could we have development without peace?' Ben agreed. 'We cannot only concentrate on freeing the children. They will never be free if there is no peace. At any time, they could be captured again. Therefore, we have to link our efforts to peace.'

The parents were asked to come up with new ideas and initiatives. One proposed to try and contact the rebels by radio. Another one opted to involve the clan leaders, rather than the politicians. 'Politicians may want to use the case for personal or political profit.' Others suggested to concentrate on the Sudan connection. 'We should try and get in touch with the President of Sudan when he visits Uganda, as is being speculated.' Most believed international pressure ought to be stepped up. An appeal should be made to the Archbishop of Canterbury to condemn the abduction, one parent threw in. After all, the Lord's Resistance Army had an office in London. 'Some of the people responsible for this abduction may be in the UK.'

The parents sat upright when the latest information was being shared. 'The girls are all in good health,' Ben said, quoting a child who had escaped two weeks earlier. 'They are being subjected to walking most of the time. So far they haven't been mistreated. We know of serious punishments of those intending to mistreat them. Sometimes they are divided in groups and assigned to the families of the leaders to help with domestic work.'

'Where are they?' somebody asked.

'At the last meeting, we said that 14 girls were with Lagony in Gulu, while 15 girls were believed to be with Lagira in Kitgum. Recent reports indicate that one group of rebels and their captives have crossed into Sudan.'

The news was met with indignation. 'What is the army doing to block the rebels' escape route?' one of the parents asked. 'What were the soldiers doing when our children were taken? The rebels could knock down the wall for hours without being disturbed!' Ben tried to stem the emotions. 'The situation is extremely complex,' he said. 'If the army doesn't intervene, they are accused of doing nothing. But if they do intervene, they are accused of killing our children. The rebels don't fight in the front line. So when the army attacks and claims victories, in reality, for us, the parents, they are defeats.'

There was a long silence. Somebody suggested the soldiers should use tear gas, so as to allow the abductees to escape. The idea was met with general approval and would be passed on to the appropriate authorities. But Ben also pointed at their own responsibility. 'We should not always condemn the army,' he said. 'We should blame ourselves too for our silence. The parents of Gulu and Kitgum should have spoken out earlier. It would have been a warning to all of us.'

There was another silence. Angelina now intervened. 'We are all in this mess together,' she said slowly and softly. 'And we have all failed to protect our children: the parents, the clan leaders, the law makers, the army, the government, the United Nations, the Organisation of African Unity. The dilemma we are facing is this: When the rebels abduct your child, how can you think of them with anything but horror? But now, your own child is living as a rebel. So if the rebels break through and demand food or information, you not only fear for yourself, you also think of your child and hope that your own child is not hungry. So, perhaps, you keep quiet and help the rebels.'

13

*And it came to pass, when men began to multiply on the face of
the earth, and daughters were born unto them, that the sons of
God saw the daughters of men that they were fair, and they
took them as wives of all which they chose. (Genesis 6, 1-2)*

At last Kony came. He had been in Juba for an operation, the rumour
went. Excitement preceded his arrival. Everybody was summoned to
the prayer ground, a big open space in the middle of the camp. Sarah
had never seen so many rebels before. Thousands were lining up, the
majority children. For the Aboke girls and the newcomers, this was
the first time they would get to see the rebel leader. Every day in the
past week Sarah had prayed that he would descend like a kind of
Messiah upon them and take them out of this nightmare.

For not long after their arrival her worst fears had come true. They
were distributed as wives to the commanders. Those who had been
brave on the battlefield were awarded an Aboke girl. Like trophies.
For Sarah, it was the most humiliating moment since the abduction.
She was given to Lakati, a man the age of her grandfather. She was his
fifth wife. Four Aboke girls were sent to Kony's home, the youngest
was only thirteen. Two were assigned to Omona.

The first time Sarah met her 'husband' he just scrutinised her for a
few seconds and walked away without saying anything. When he finally
talked to her, he only said: 'You are now a soldier like me. You must
survive on your own.' The night she was called into his hut was the
darkest night of her life. There was no way she could refuse. If she
resisted, she would be killed. While it was happening, she had already
wiped it from her memory. This was a part of the story she didn't want
to remember nor find the words for.

The prayer ceremony around her had started. The commanders
emerged first. They were dressed in white clothes and sprinkled the
soil with water from a jerrycan. There was a lot of cheering and singing

and clapping from the recruits. Then, surrounded by several circles of guards, Kony appeared. He walked steadily, his eyes flicking sideways. Sarah was surprised. She had expected a huge man with charismatic features, somebody who would strike you at first sight. But this slender soldier in uniform didn't look any different from most men she knew. He was even younger than some of his commanders. Only when he started talking did she understand why some people attributed magical powers to him. He was an excellent speaker. Like a president. Or rather, as he constantly referred to God and the Bible, like a bishop. The rebels looked up at him with a mixture of fear and awe. Sarah listened attentively, trying to understand the Acholi. She gathered that he vowed to take over Uganda and rule it by the Ten Commandments of Moses. All his acts were inspired by the Holy Spirit, Lakwena. 'We don't kill. We fight for a good cause, just like in the Bible. Out of self-defence.' The recruits could not dream of going home before they had defeated Museveni's army.

Sarah hoped all the time that he would say something about the Aboke girls. After all, he had personally ordered their abduction. But to her disappointment, he made no mention of them. While the singing and cheering resumed, a kind of panic arose in her. Escaping from Sudan seemed almost impossible. Rebel units constantly marched to and from the border. Moreover, there were several Arab camps between Aru and the border with Uganda. The Arab soldiers, they had been told, caught the children who tried to escape to bring them back to the camp, where they would be killed. The Ugandan army could not come and rescue them here either. They were way into Sudan.

Even escaping from the camp would be difficult. Aru was organised in such a way that everybody controlled everybody. There were four brigades: Stockree, Sania, Gilver and Kony's headquarters – Control Altar. Each brigade was led by a commander and divided into smaller units. These were broken up into 'families,' consisting of a soldier, his wife or wives and their children: recruits under thirteen or children born in the movement.

Was there no way back? Sarah wondered. Was she doomed to stay for the rest of her life in this hot, unforgiving desert, cut off from her family and her motherland? She looked out at the remorseless emptiness of the surrounding space and felt suddenly terribly alone. Even her schoolmates she hardly got to see nowadays. Each was now confined to her 'family.'

In her own family, she couldn't find much sympathy either. Her co-wives had received her with open hostility. Some were older, some younger than her. Two had made it to commander. They had all been abducted once, but now they had 'adapted' to their new life and seemed to be proud of it. Sarah had become the target of their abuse and pestering: because she was stubborn and refused to fetch water from the river, six miles away. And because she was a girl of Aboke. Once, when the Aboke girls were mentioned on the radio, she was beaten. 'You must be very special to the Government of Uganda,' her co-wives screamed. 'One day we will take you to the bush and kill you.'

Lakati, her husband, beat her too. It was part of the daily routine. In the morning, she and the recruits assigned to their unit got a thrashing with his stick, so that they would 'accept' their situation and never think of escaping again. Oh, how she despised that old man! In turn, the wives had to spend the night with him. There was no love or tenderness involved. It was but the act of an animal. While the singing and cheering around her grew louder, Sarah let herself sink ever deeper into a dark hole out of which there seemed to be no return.

***

Norman pretended to be listening. Lakati was explaining how to set landmines and launch mortars. But Norman knew everything already. He could distinguish anti-tank mines from anti-personnel mines. He could tell the difference between 60 and 82-mm mortar grenades. And he knew all the guns by name. There were RPGs, B10, SPGs, SMGs, LMGs, KPMs and SAM7 missiles. The weapons all came from the Sudanese armed forces, just as everything else: the radio transmitters and solar panels, the trucks that brought the food from Juba, as well as the pick-up and the motorcycle for Kony's personal use.

The relationship between Kony and the Arabs was not very clear to Norman. The Arabs often came to the camp to trade. The rebels then exchanged charcoal or stolen goods from Uganda for food or uniforms. Norman also traded *bangi* with them, a kind of marijuana that he cultivated privately, knowing the Arabs were crazy about it. In exchange he got soap or sugar. Once in a while they went and fought with the Arabs against the local Dinka, who had their own army, the SPLA.

He didn't know what the war in Sudan was about. All he knew was that the Dinka were fierce fighters. Their only disadvantage was that they were so tall. They fought lying down or from trenches. The smallest LRA rebels - those who could move unseen through the bush - were then sent to the trenches to shoot as many Dinka as possible and clear out fast, before they were hit.

During one of those battles, Norman had almost been killed. Kony had ordered them to attack a big SPLA camp and to return with the private parts of the enemy. He and his fellow fighters had surprised the Dinka in their sleep, very early in the morning. The Dinka soldiers threw themselves into the trenches. One soldier was hidden behind a small bush, firing at Norman non-stop as he came running at a very high speed. He knew in such cases it was allowed to use the bomb. So he snatched the grenade out of his pocket, pulled the fuse and threw it into the trench as he was only a few yards away. A huge explosion followed. One of his fellow rebels later returned to cut off the private parts of the dead.

The Arabs were cowards, really, Norman thought. Without Kony's fighters, they would not win a single battle. Because they were afraid, and they could not stand the heat of the sun. Whenever the Dinka attacked at noon, they just ran away and left it to Kony's fighters to beat off the attackers. 'When the recruits die, it is not a big problem,' he had once overheard his commander say. 'There are many children in Uganda.'

Kony himself seldom took part in the fighting. Norman had seen him only once on the battlefield, in Uganda. He fired at a *Mamba*, but he missed it and ran off. Mostly when the fighting erupted, his escorts would lead him to safety and he would only show up again after the battle, to count the casualties. He was not a real soldier, Norman reflected bitterly. He made the abducted children fight for him while he was enjoying a comfortable life in Sudan. He had a compound almost as big as a landing strip, and lots of wives. At least thirty. It was said that some of them were living in houses in Juba, which he visited from time to time. He also had many children, all born in the movement. One of his sons was five and he was already a corporal.

Kony was crazy about children. That's what he told Norman during the one and only time they had met face to face. Norman was digging his garden when Kony suddenly appeared. He pointed at the kids playing in his compound and said: 'I love small children. I am going to demand all the children of the commanders.'

Some claimed that Kony had magical powers. Norman didn't know what to think of that. There was certainly something strange about the man. During prayers, he could talk for up to eight hours without stopping or sitting down. And he predicted battles which indeed took place. It was a strange religion Kony adhered to. He prayed to the God of the Christians on Sundays, reciting the rosary and quoting the Bible, but he also prayed on Fridays, like the Muslims. He celebrated Christmas, but he also fasted for 30 days during Ramadhan and prohibited the consumption of pork. And then there was all that talk of the spirits, which stemmed from the traditional Acholi culture.

Norman could not figure out where the other laws came from. They could, for example, not fight with food in their mouth or steal when they were not ordered to steal. They had to respect stones and water, because - as Kony claimed - magical powers emerged from them. They were not allowed to sit or urinate on stones, knock them against each other or use them to clean their toes. They had to take off their shoes and refrain from shouting when crossing a river and they could not relieve themselves in a stream.

But Kony's prayers were mainly like political meetings. Military songs were sung and Kony talked of Museveni's evil plans to wipe out the Acholi people. At the end, the rebel leader would give his orders for the coming week. These were always the same. Units were selected to go and fight the SPLA or the Ugandan army. Those who were sent to Uganda were also told to loot medicines and food, burn houses and punish those civilians who failed to respect the rules. For riding a bicycle, the punishment was hacking off a leg or an arm. Those who accidentally crossed their path had their ears or lips cut off or their eyes plucked out. And the punishment for working on Fridays or breeding pigs was death.

During the lastest prayers, Kony had told them that they would leave for Uganda on the fourth of January. They were to punish the people of Kitgum, because a group of children from that area had escaped. He suspected them of having revealed the location of arms caches to the Ugandan army. 'Nobody in Kitgum should be left alive,' he had shouted. 'Those old enough to differentiate between good and bad should all be killed, even the old ones. Because they are stupid, and they don't listen to what I say.' Then he had said something which struck Norman. 'I could kill all Acholi and put their heads on the road. For I will deliver a new Acholi generation!' At the end, Kony had selected some recruits from Kitgum district and made them lie down. Then he had ordered the rebels to beat them up. 'If that stroke can kill them, it is even better!' he had encouraged his aides, who hit so hard that some of the victims didn't move anymore.

Norman looked up as Lakati was finishing his instructions. Four units would leave tomorrow morning for Uganda, the commander said. Support was one of them. In a way Norman was relieved he was to go back to Uganda. It would give him a chance to escape. The cleansing ceremomy around him started. As usual, before leaving for a big fight, prayers were said and rituals performed. 'God, give us the power to defeat the enemy,' everybody prayed. Then the commanders set about pouring water over them, in order to wash away their sins so that they would be able to repulse the enemy. Like his fellow fighters, Norman was clapping frantically. He felt the little stone knock against his wrist. He was wearing it for protection, just like the little bottle filled with holy water around his neck. 'The problems we are facing will end in heaven, where God is', he sang loudly with the others.

As the ceremony grew wilder, a thought suddenly sprang to his mind. If tomorrow was the fourth of January, it meant that New Year's Day had already passed. And they hadn't overthrown the government of Uganda. Now he was convinced it was all nonsense. Kony would never be the president of Uganda. It was as if suddenly the spell was broken. Nothing could deter him any longer: once back in Uganda, he would escape!

14

For then will I turn to the people a pure language, that they may all call upon the name of the Lord, to serve him with one consent. (Zephaniah 3,9)

Ellen avoided looking at her schoolmates. 'I'm not going to Sudan' she whispered, trying to control her fury. 'I will never become Omona's wife. Never!' Lucy, one of the two wives in her family, had blurted it out that morning during one of their many fights. 'Fortunately, I will be rid of you tomorrow. We are going to meet Omona's unit. You will be given to him as a wife and he will take you to Sudan.'

Ellen fiercely soaked her cassava bread in the gravy. 'I am not staying here another day. Today or tomorrow I will escape. Will you come with me?' Esther looked around in alarm to make sure nobody was listening. The four Aboke girls stayed in different units but they ate their meals together. It was one of those rare moments when they could exchange some news.

'We cannot escape together,' Pamela said quietly. 'It would be too obvious if four girls disappeared at the same time.' Ellen put a piece of cassava in her mouth. 'Maybe I can go alone,' she mumbled, chewing her food. 'You too can try your chance. Go your own way. All of us.'

'Ellen, please, don't leave me behind.' Ellen looked up and met the pleading eyes of little Esther. She feared the girl's outburst would attract the commanders' attention. 'All right,' she said soothingly. 'If I get the chance, I'll take you with me.'

She got up and returned to her unit. Since she had been transferred to Anywar's family, she had constantly been quarrelling with his first wife, Lucy, who was in her early 20s and already a second lieutenant. Ellen systematically ignored Lucy's orders, which made her furious. Almost daily, she was beaten. 'I will shoot you and say that it was a mistake,' Lucy would scream. Or 'I will stab you to death and claim that you tried to escape.'

Lucy had been in the movement since the very beginning. She had been kidnapped by the followers of Alice Lakwena in 1988, at the age of 12. Later she had fled with Alice to Kenya. But in the 1990s she came back to join Kony. 'Alice Lakwena started to misbehave,' she told Ellen one evening. 'The power left her and went to Kony.'

With Margaret, Anywar's second wife, it was different. Margaret was not much older than Ellen and would only beat her if she was told to. In fact, Ellen quite liked her, although there were many things about her she didn't understand. Margaret stoically tolerated Lucy's whims and underwent the beatings without complaining. She also believed in the spirit of Lakwena and was convinced of the rightness of Kony's actions. She never wanted to go back home, she often said. Ellen couldn't make out whether she meant it or was just pretending. If there was anything she had learnt in these past months, it was not to trust anybody. For trusting the wrong person could mean death.

Ellen tried to come close to her. When she was sure Lucy couldn't hear them, she asked: 'Margaret, suppose you were free tomorrow, would you go back to your parents?' The girl stared at her for a moment, puzzled. 'Even at gunpoint I would not go home,' she then answered firmly. 'Because the army would kill me, and also my relatives. Besides, if the rebels found me at home, they would destroy my village.' She peered at Ellen, as if reading her mind, and then shook her head. 'Really, Ellen, there is no way.'

Anywar seemed to suspect something. Or would Lucy have been complaining? He summoned the four Aboke girls.

'Ellen, are you happy these days?' he asked. But she refused to answer. He turned to Jacky and Pamela and repeated the question. They both nodded.

'And you, Esther. Are you happy?'

The girl didn't answer either. He turned back to Ellen, angrily waving his finger at her. 'Ellen, you are bad-mannered. And you are misleading Esther. You are making life impossible for everybody!'

Ellen looked down, her lips sealed. Only one thought ran through her mind: Tomorrow I'll be gone. Scold as much as you want, tomorrow I'll be gone!

Luckily, the sign for departure was given and Anywar left them alone. Dusk was falling. Their figures cast long shadows which loomed in the last pale reach of the sun. In order not to miss the meeting with Omona's group, they would walk all through the night, without sleeping. Ellen felt her determination grow with every step. The thought of becoming Omona's wife seemed to have given her extraordinary courage. She knew the risks involved in trying to escape. But then at least she would be spared the shame of becoming the wife of a commander older than her father. When the birds started singing and the first light split the night sky, she was all ready to die. She turned to Esther.

'Today is my day.'

'Do your utmost to take me with you,' the girl pleaded.

The four of them marched behind each other.

'Why are you walking together?' Anywar asked and he slapped them on the back. 'Or are you planning something?' They dispersed. Ellen now closed the line. As they walked through a banana grove, she suddenly bumped into an old man who was hiding behind a tree. Instantly, she looked around to check if anybody else had seen him. She knew what happened to people who accidentally crossed their path. Once they had met a peasant returning from his fields. The rebels grabbed him and beat him on the back with a panga. Then they used a bundle of burning straw to singe the wounds, while the man screamed in agony. Another time she had seen villagers whose mouths had been sealed with padlocks and the keys thrown away. 'Go and ask Museveni to try and open them,' the rebels had screamed.

'Don't be afraid,' she whispered to the old man who had fallen on his knees in front of her. 'Just stay here. Nobody else will find you as I am the last in the line.' But the man went on pleading, his hands folded. 'Please, forgive me. Don't report me.'

'I won't,' she reassured him. 'I am a captive myself. Just stay here.'

She left him still sitting, his hands folded. It was nearly nine o'clock: time for the radio contact. As the commander got busy installing the solar panel, a helicopter suddenly appeared on the skyline. To Ellen it was like a sign from God.

As everybody ran for cover, she grabbed Esther's hand and pulled her to a small circle of grass under a tree. It was the only place that had not been burnt in preparation for the new planting season. Ellen had spotted the place immediately. Nobody would even imagine anyone could hide in there. They threw themselves in the tall grass and lay waiting. After a while, the helicopter turned away. Now there was only the sound of the radio left, and the voice of the commander. When the communication was over, the commander clapped his hands, the sign for moving. Ellen felt her friend trembling next to her.

'Let's pretend we are sleeping,' she whispered. 'After all, we have walked all night. If they find us, we just say sorry, we fell asleep, we didn't know it was time to leave.'

Esther was breathing heavily beside her. The minutes seemed to last forever. Ellen knew the rebels couldn't lose much time looking for them. The appointment with Omona's group was set for midday. There were footsteps nearby. She held her breath, but the steps passed by. It must have been the guards, she thought. They always walked in a circle of half a mile around the group to check if any soldiers were coming. Motionlessly they waited, until the birds settled back in the trees and nature went all quiet.

Then, at last, Ellen dared sit up. She told Esther to take off her slippers and to leave the luggage behind: a jerrycan, a cooking pan, some plates and a bag of baking flour. 'Now, follow me.' They started running in the direction where Ellen had heard a *Mamba* pass the night before. She knew that was the road to Gulu. From time to time, she looked back to see whether Esther was keeping up. Suddenly they were alarmed by a rustling sound. Ellen looked around in fear. Then she spotted the old man she had come across in the morning. Again he fell on his knees. But she quickly gestured him to stand up. 'Haven't I told you that I am a captive myself? Now we have escaped. Quickly, show us the way to Palenga training centre.'

The old man wanted to lead them but he was too slow. 'We have to hurry,' she said. 'The rebels might come after us. Just give us the directions.' He explained the way and they started running again. It was as if freedom had given them wings. They almost flew over the burnt fields and through the banana plantations, for hours, until the main road lay in front of them. A man passed by on a bicycle. They stopped him and explained that they had escaped from the rebels. The man, who appeared to be a pastor, immediately understood what was going on. 'Come on,' he gestured and they climbed on the back of his bicycle. He took them straight to the army post in Palenga. As they entered the barracks, Ellen thought she was dreaming. The soldiers welcomed them and asked them all kinds of questions, but she couldn't concentrate. Only at night, when she woke up and saw Esther lying next to her, did she realise the nightmare was over. 'It's really true,' little Esther whispered. 'We have made it. We are free!' Ellen let her tears flow freely, tears of relief and pain and endless happiness.

Joseph Kony, the leader of the Lord's Resistance Army

Hundreds of thousands of people in northern Uganda have fled to refugee camps or 'protected villages.'

Sister Rachele and Angelina - the chairperson of the Concerned Parents Association: they never give up

Sister Rachele, the deputy headmistress of St Mary's, Aboke, has spared no effort both inside and outside Uganda in endless search for her girls

Sister Rachele at Nisitu women's camp in South Sudan, accompanied by Sudanese officers

Sister Rachele and Ben Pere interrogate three girls at Kony's headquarters in South Sudan. Monica (far right) was killed shortly after this picture was taken

Norman (third left) is queuing for food at World Vision reception centre

New arrivals at World Vision reception centre in Gulu

Sister Rachele campaigning for the release of her children in The Netherlands

Sister Rachele had an audience with Pope John Paul II in December 1998

Simon's arm was cut off because he had run away. As a rebel soldier started cutting the left arm, he was stopped by his officer and reminded of the instruction to chop off the right arm. He then cut the right arm. Simon was left on the road and nearly bled to death before he was found and taken to hospital.

Hundreds of thousands of people in northern Uganda have fled to refugee camps or 'protected villages.'

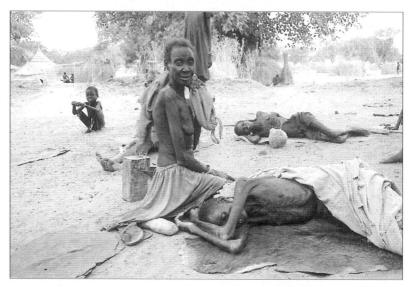

The war in Sudan has already claimed more than one million lives. Human rights groups talk about a deliberate policy of extermination of the South

The Dinka people in South Sudan have armed themselves to protect their villages

Sister Alba, the headmistress of St Mary's, Aboke

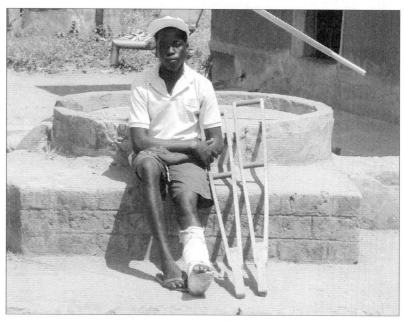

Charles was abducted in February 2000 and got a bullet in the leg when the rebels were abushed by government troops

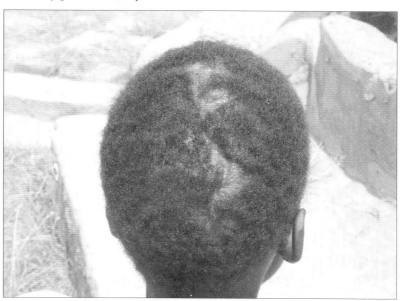

Walter was hit three times with an axe on the back of the head and thrown into the bush. After two weeks he was rescued by government troops and taken to hospital in Kitgum

The Italian Comboni Sisters are striving to provide some of the country's best education at St Mary's, Aboke

Sister Rachele shows how the rebels got into the dormitory. The windows have in the meantime been closed

Victims of the LRA rebels: Ayako (48), her eye was removed with a wire, her husband and two children were killed and her house burnt

Carcy (25), her upper lip and nose were cut because she was moving on the road. She was forced to eat them. If she had cried, her neck would have been cut by a small boy holding a panga. Nine other people were tortured in this way

Wilson (63), his ears were cut. Six other people were killed in this incident

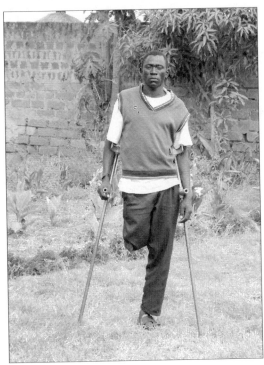

George was abducted, for 4 years he fought the SPLM eleven times. During a battle in 1997 he got several bullets in the leg. He was taken to Omdurman military hospital in Khartoum where his leg was amputated. He escaped from the hospital and hid in an Islamic mission for 2 years until he was rescued by UNICEF officials and repatriated to Uganda in September 2000

Recruits of the LRA have to steal their food from the Dinka people in South Sudan who are themselves starving

An SPLA camp in South Sudan

15

Weep save for him that goeth away: for he shall return no more,
nor see his native country... but he shall die in the place whither
they have led him captive. (Jeremiah 22, 10-12)

The intelligence officer in Gulu got up to greet Sister Rachele. He was an exceptionally tall man. When he embraced her, her head only reached his chest. She introduced the rest of the delegation: Angelina Atyam, Ben Pere and Dr Olyet, all parents of abducted Aboke girls and members of the board of the Concerned Parents Association. The officer invited them to sit down. 'What can I do for you, Sister?'

She formulated her question carefully. 'Is there a possibility of rescuing our girls? Do you have any information on their whereabouts?'

The officer's answer was formal: 'They are in Sudan.'

Sister Rachele plucked nervously at her bag. 'We were hoping, since we heard some groups are around, that perhaps some of the girls are still here.'

The officer shook his head. 'No, we have tried to infiltrate the remaining groups to find out if the girls were there. But the information I get is that the Aboke girls are not there.' And then, with more emphasis: 'The girls are all in Sudan, Sister. They are in Aru, Kony's camp.'

'Do you think it would be possible for us to reach that camp?'

He looked at her in amazement. 'Sister, I don't know. Sudan is a different country. I don't have any authority over that territory!'

'Are the children all alive and in good health?' Angelina now intervened.

The officer turned to her. 'Their wellbeing depends on the commander they were given to.' He coughed. 'All these girls have been given to commanders. We know that at least one has been given to Kony.'

Rachele's eyes filled with tears. She got up and looked straight at the officer. 'Can you not send them a message to tell them that we want to go there to get our girls?'

'But you can't do that if you don't have any connections there.'

'You said you have information. How did you get that information? Can't you send them a message by the same way and tell them that we want to go there and bring our girls back?'

He shook his head in disbelief. Ben had got up and was standing next to her. 'The international community should come and confront them,' he said. 'The international community must do something!'

'These questions should be put to the international organisations. I only deal with the military option.' The officer glanced sideways at Sister Rachele and added: 'An option the sister doesn't want.'

'It's not the answer', she murmured.

'It is the answer, Sister. To avoid any further abductions, the only solution is the military option.'

'Why can't peace negotiationsbe a solution?'

He shrugged. 'Negotiations have failed.'

There was nothing more to say. They left the military headquarters and proceeded to the prison at the back.

They had heard that two LRA commanders had just been captured. One of them had been involved in the abduction of the Aboke girls. The boy, a young fellow with uncombed hair and a wild look, recognised Sister Rachele immediately. The conversation was difficult.

'Are the girls given to the men of their own free choice?' Angelina asked.

'No, they are given by order,' the boy mumbled.

'You mean they are forced?'

The second commander, who looked a lot older, intervened.

'Yes, they are forced. Even me, if I wanted a girl, I just took her. They have no choice. If they refuse, they will be accused of trying to escape and they will be killed.'

Sister Rachele felt the tears welling up in her eyes again. But Ben Pere pressed on.

'Do they take the girls only for sex? Could there be any other reasons?'

The boy shook his head. 'No, it's the only reason.'

Nobody spoke as they walked back. Sister Rachele's face was distorted in pain. The stories were always a torment to herself and the parents. And yet they wanted to know. That was the aim of their association: to gather information in order to be able to lobby more efficiently. A strong bond had grown between the sisters and the parents, united as they were in their grief. When one lost courage, the others would cheer him or her up again. There had always been a spark of hope, something to hold on to.

It was five months ago now since the thirty girls were taken, and six had made it back home. The last one, Grace, escaped a month ago from Kitgum. Their escape stories had been unbelievable. Grace had fled into the river during an attack by the government troops. She had managed to cling to a bundle of reeds and had hidden in the water for hours, while other rebels were drowning around her. When the fighting stopped, she came out, only to find herself being shot at by a column of soldiers on the other bank of the river. An old man who had tried to cross the river died next to her. She got away and wandered around for another twenty-four hours before she found somebody to help her. Before Grace, it was the return of Ellen and Esther that had caused great joy.

To Sister Rachele each escape was a moment of delight: another child in safety, another life saved. She was counting down: twenty-four left. But the moments of joy were always shortlived. For the stories of the escapees made her fear the worst for those who stayed behind. She was now convinced that they had all been taken to Sudan and distributed as wives to Kony's top commanders. Getting them out of these men's grip seemed an almost impossible task.

The attacks meanwhile continued unabated. In January, the rebels had again invaded in big numbers and seriously ravaged Kitgum district. In less than a week, over 400 civilians had been killed, hacked and clubbed to death, and an unknown number of children had again been abducted. Fifty thousand people had fled the area, bringing the total number of internally displaced persons to over 400,000, almost half the population of northern Uganda. The rebels had also planted mines on all major roads. Apart from a constant stream of the wounded from the war and the rebels' terror tactics, Lacor, Gulu's main hospital, also had to deal with an increasing number of mine victims. Playing children, in particular, fell prey to these vicious hidden weapons that crippled them in a split second. The army had subsequently gone on a counter-offensive, claiming to have killed 50 rebels, including Commander Otim.

There were more alarming developments. A second rebel movement led by Juma Oris, mainly consisting of ex-soldiers of Idi Amin, had announced in the press that it had joined the Lord's Resistance Army. They had united, they said, 'to overthrow the government together'.

Also in Apac district, where her school was located, there had been new reports of rebel movements and abductions. Although the school was now permanently guarded by 60 soldiers, Sister Rachele still felt insecure. Fear haunted her in the long, sleepness nights as she lay staring into the dark, getting up to ask the watchman if everything was all right, then going back to bed, staring into the dark again and listening to the sounds of the night. Some of the girls who had escaped even changed schools for fear that the rebels would come looking for them. But in their new schools, they had been branded 'rebels' and 'Kony's wives'.

Sister Rachele took a deep breath as she entered Museveni's office at the military headquarters. It was the first time that the parents were going to meet the president. Angelina was rather sceptical. 'He promised that our children would never be taken to Sudan,' she said. 'But now they are in Sudan. They are dressed in military uniforms and carry guns. These are the children who are sent to Uganda to die at the frontline. And what is he going to do about it?' But Sister Rachele believed that Museveni did care. So many times, she had gone to him for help. He had always found time in his busy schedule, listening and encouraging her and coming up with new ideas and initiatives. During her last visit, a week ago, he even promised to raise the matter with Kofi Annan, the Secretary General of the United Nations.

The president received them with a promising smile. After the introductions, he handed them a letter he had personally written to Kofi Annan. 'Mr Secretary General,' it said,

Reference to our telephone conversation, I would like to furnish you with the details of the 24 school girls from St Mary's, Aboke in northern Uganda who were kidnapped by the bandits belonging to the Kony group supported by the Sudan government... The 30 school girls are part of thousands that have been abducted into Sudan by agents of the Sudan government... We reserve the right to take all legitimate measures to end this criminality against our civilian population, especially the children. If the Sudan government wants to destabilise Uganda, they should advise their agents to attack the army but not the civilians.

At the end he urged the secretary general 'to cause the Sudan Government to release all the abductees currently in Aru, Southern Sudan, especially the 24 school girls.'

Sister Rachele carefully folded the letter and put it in her bag. This was a big step forward, she thought. Ben addressed the president: 'Your Excellency, we have been informed that a high level meeting between Uganda and Sudan will take place tomorrow, with the mediation of Iran. Do you think there is a possibility for us to be there and present our case?'

Museveni pondered for a while. 'I don't see why not,' he then replied. He called his secretary and asked him to reserve four seats in his helicopter. Then he turned to Sister Rachele: 'I suggest that you give the Iranian minister my letter to the UN Secretary General.'

The following morning they joined President Museveni in his helicopter. The meeting took place in Sambiya Lodge, a guest house in African style in the middle of Murchison Park. In fact, this was only a preliminary meeting, Museveni explained. 'The real talks start only tomorrow in Entebbe.' The other delegates had already arrived. Among them were the ministers for foreign affairs of Iran, Malawi, Uganda and the under-secretary for foreign affairs of Sudan.

Sister Rachele and the parents were told to wait outside the meeting room, while Museveni entered to greet the representatives and open the talks. At last he came out and they entered. Ben spoke first. He introduced the delegation and told them about the abduction. 'I suggest we listen to Sister Rachele who followed the rebels', he said, giving her the floor. She told the delegates about her pursuit and her visit to Nairobi. Angelina was to say something about the Concerned Parents Association, but she burst into tears and could not utter a word. Dr Olyet came to her help. He explained the context of the conflict and stressed that the children were the main victims of the war. In the end, Sister Rachele gave the Iranian minister Museveni's letter to the UN. The excellencies had been listening attentively. Then the Malawian foreign minister spoke. He expressed shock and concern about the abduction of children and their use as soldiers and emphasised that respect for children was inherent in African culture. The Iranian minister promised to put Museveni's letter on the agenda of their meeting. The Sudanese under-secretary spoke last. He said he knew nothing about the 'incident' but promised to inform his government.

Satisfied, they left the room. Again Sister Rachele felt they had done something useful, they had talked to people who had the power to do something. They were even invited to stay for lunch and the atmosphere was most agreeable. But the following day, back at St Mary's, they waited in vain for a reaction. At the press conference following the talks in Entebbe, no word was said about the Aboke girls.

16

Behold, I will bring evil upon this people, even the fruit of their thoughts, because they have not heartened unto my words, nor to my law, but rejected it. (Jeremiah 6, 19)

Norman felt sick and disgusted. It had been a successful operation as far as the commanders were concerned. But to him it was a total disaster, a horrifying and senseless bloodbath. No villagers had been spared during their murderous trek through Kitgum district. Norman had been sent to Lukung and Padibe. First, they surrounded the homesteads. Then they stormed the huts, killing everyone old enough to differentiate between good and bad and abducting the others. Men, women and young people were tied and made to lie down, after which they were stabbed, stoned or beaten to death with bayonets and sticks. The old were butchered where they were sitting. And those who tried to run away were shot. But most people did not resist. They were paralysed by fear.

For several days they had moved from village to village. However, as word of their advance spread, they found fewer and fewer people in the homesteads. Then they were split into small groups of ten. Each rebel was ordered to abduct four children: two for the movement and two for himself. Norman still recalled the fearful eyes of the boys he had captured himself. He had felt so bad that he let one escape. Fortunately, nobody knew he was the one who let the boy flee.

And now they were on their way back to Sudan, with about 200 new recruits. Norman checked his gun, the seven magazines of bullets and the grenades. They had made a good fighter of him. He would now turn the guns against them, if he had to.

They were making good progress. The Sudanese border was only some 30 miles away. Norman had chosen his moment carefully. In the dimming evening light, he sneaked away in the tangled thicket. As if by miracle, he found a big rock and hid in the fissure underneath. He waited anxiously, trying to stem his gasp. Escaping was giving yourself up, he knew. But he didn't care. He had reached a point at which he accepted that death was better than this kind of life. He heard the rebels search for him. 'Have you found him?' one of them asked. His heart was pounding so loudly that he feared they would hear it. Then somebody nearby found the fuse of his grenade. His breath stopped. He expected to be dragged out any moment. But nobody thought about looking under the rock. 'Let's go back,' he heard the rebels say. He was on the alert. It could be a trick to make him come out. He lay motionless under the rock, suddenly feeling overwhelmed by exhaustion. Slowly but surely, he dozed off.

It was light when Norman woke up. He lay still for a while, listening intently to make sure that the rebels had left. Then he hauled himself out of his hiding place and started running in the opposite direction, back to Kitgum. The ammunition weighed like lead. But his main concern was food. His stomach was growling non-stop. At last, when the sun was high, a circle of huts emerged in the distance. The homestead was deserted, except for a few chickens. He grabbed one and slaughtered it. But he didn't dare make a fire for fear that the smoke would give him away. He decided to wait for darkness. As he was assessing his situation, he suddenly realised he had no water. The only source he knew was the river back where he came from. Dare he turn back? His thirst was greater than his fear, however. He raced all the way back, filled his jerrycan and was safely in the homestead again before dark.

Satisfied with himself, he installed himself in a hut and started making a fire. As he was fanning the flames, he suddenly heard a sound outside which he would recognise from among a thousand others. Gumboots! The smoke must have betrayed him! He stiffened, but only for a second. Then he grabbed his gun and hid himself behind the door.

'Norman, come out!'

It was the voice of a boy of his unit. Through a crack in the fence, he saw that the rebels had posted themselves in front of the door, their guns at the ready. Norman trembled all over his body. He knew he was no match for the group outside. Moreover, he saw them lighting a bundle of grass to burn down the hut. It was now or never. He cocked his rifle and pointed the barrel through the opening of the door. The rebels leaped back in fear. He took advantage of the confusion and stormed out, shooting wildly. Some of the rebels fled, others fired back. He heard the bullets whistle over his head as he ducked into the thicket, running through the bush like a hunted animal. He expected to fall down any moment, but miraculously he kept on running, only one thought thumping like a refrain in his head: If they catch me, I'm dead.

It was pitch-dark when he finally stopped. He listened intently in all directions and concluded that the rebels had given up the pursuit, probably because they now knew he was armed. Hunger made him feel weak and weary. He found a tree and posted himself against it. And before he knew, he dozed off again.

The first sunshine on his face awoke him. His stomach felt tied in knots and his head was light. In the bright light of the morning, he took his gun and went in search of food. As he approached a homestead, one of the villagers spotted him and everybody ran off before he could even speak to them. Maybe he should throw away his gun, he pondered. But how could he then defend himself against any rebels who crossed his path? As he stood there, considering what to do, he felt the ground under his feet shake again. He looked around in alarm. The huts didn't seem a safe hiding place. There was only a termite hill nearby. He quickly took cover behind it. As the group drew nearer, he saw it was a unit of the Gilver Brigade. They roamed around in the homestead for a while, looking for food. Some rebels came very close to the termite hill. Norman curled up, trying as much as possible to make himself invisible, but they were too busy picking the fruit in the tree above them. He heard them taste the fruit, then spit it out and throw it away. At last, they continued their march.

It took a long time before Norman dared to come out again. He tried the fruit of the tree, anything to dampen the gnawing hunger in his stomach, but it was too sour. His attention was suddenly raised by the buzzing of bees. Where there are bees, he reasoned, there is honey and he started following them. He found their nest and instantly put his hand into it. The bees came swarming out, stinging him in great numbers. He shrieked and ran away. Only later did he discover that he had lost his gun, probably while he was shaking off the bees. Going back was too risky. He decided to wait until the heat had subsided. Maybe by then the rebels would have left the area as well.

Late in the afternoon he went back to collect his gun and left. But he had lost all sense of direction. He drew a map of Uganda in the sand as he remembered it from his Geography lessons, then compared it to the position of the sun and decided that Kitgum must be in front of him. He passed another empty homestead and to his relief, he found a few chickens. He instantly killed one, took out the intestines and – his previous experience in mind – ate it raw. The last of the sun was fading from the far-off plains as he got up again. His third night in freedom. And still he was wandering around in this hostile land where everyone was an enemy.

He summoned up his courage and headed for the next homestead. But a dog started barking loudly and for fear that it would alarm the rebels, he ran off again. He had left the thicket and was now walking on the main road so as to proceed faster. A light bundle penetrated the darkness in front of him. Even before he heard the sound of the engine, he knew it was a *Mamba*. The army always patrolled the main roads. He hid on the roadside waiting for the armoured vehicle to pass. Later on, it was the droning of a tank that made him look for cover. For a moment he thought the soldiers had spotted him as the tank slowed down, then rolled past him at a snail's pace. He decided to take a short rest at the side of the road. He lay awake for a long time, wishing that somebody, somewhere would have mercy upon him.

The next morning he was woken up by the sound of people. A few villagers on bicycles were coming his way. This is my chance, Norman thought, as he hid in the grass. When they were close enough, he sprang in front of their bicycles, pointing his gun at them. 'Stop or I shoot!' The villagers immediately stopped and raised their hands. 'It's all right. I have escaped from the rebels,' he tried to reassure them. 'Can you take me to the local councillor?'

From the look on their faces, Norman could tell that they didn't trust him. 'First throw away your gun and bullets,' one of the villagers shouted. He hesitated. 'OK, if you want my gun, let us then go together to the local councillor.'

They agreed and he climbed on to the carrier of a bicycle. But instead of the councillor's house, they took him to the nearest protected camp and handed him over to a soldier. Norman's appearance caused great commotion. The refugees gathered around him, studying him and his gun closely. Their eyes were hostile.

'You killed our relatives!' one shouted.

'Let's kill him!' another screamed.

The soldier tried to disperse the crowd. Norman clung to his gun. When somebody starts beating me up, I'll shoot them all, he thought. At last the soldier succeeded in calming down the crowd and Norman was led to the commander's office. In the barracks he was disarmed and turned in the uniform and boots, stolen from the government troops. He was given a pair of trousers and a shirt of the home guards. The commander started questioning him: where he came from, what kind of weapons the rebels used, where his fellow soldiers were and how many camps there were between the border and Aru.

Later in the afternoon, two more children who had escaped from the rebels were brought in. Norman knew one of them, a boy he had abducted from Kitgum. They greeted each other like old friends and Norman took care of him as if he were a brother. The second boy, Victor, had a bullet in his arm. That night, he lay crying next to Norman. 'Stop crying or I won't let any of you live,' one of the guards shouted.

But he let them live. Oddly enough, Norman didn't know whether he should feel happy about that. He was terrified to go home, to the village where the rebels could trace him; to his parents who had not been able to protect him; to a world that had done nothing, nothing at all for them.

17

*He brought famine upon them and his zeal made their numbers
small. By the word of the Lord he shut up the sky and three
times called down fire. (Ecclesiasticus 48, 2-3)*

Nature was harsh and inhospitable in this land where the sun burnt
upon endless miles of sand. Even the leopards only emerged at night.
Sarah looked out over the flat and featureless landscape as she walked
behind her 'husband,' Commander Lakati. She felt so weak that she
could hardly carry her gun. Hungry. She was always hungry. It had
brought out a survival instinct in her which she had never realised was
there. Lakati was right. Hunger had taught her how to shoot. She
couldn't remember exactly when she had been given this gun. One
day all newcomers were summoned by Raska, the commander of
Stockree, and guns had been distributed. Raska had explained how to
assemble and load the weapon, but they had never learnt how to fire it.
'I cannot shoot,' she later told Lakati and he laughed and replied:
'Hunger will teach you how to shoot!'

How true these words had proved. Her worst enemy, she had come
to learn, was not man but nature. As the dry season proceeded and the
fields no longer yielded anything, the food stocks began to run out.
Once in a while the Sudanese army brought them some sorghum and
beans, but the bulk of it was claimed by the commanders. The recruits
had to survive on potato leaves, insects and roots, which caused
diarrhoea. Worse even was the water shortage. The river had dried up
and they were forced to dig with their fingers in the *waddi* to try and
collect a few dropfuls.

The first time Sarah found a recruit lying dead along the path to the
river, she had been shocked. But now she had grown used to it. Even
when somebody was sitting against a tree, as if resting, she knew that
person was dead, dehydrated. She had also grown used to the dead in
the camp. Every morning people were buried, killed by hunger, thirst

or disease. Medicines and health care were minimal. Except, of course, for the commanders who were sent to the military hospital in Juba or Khartoum when they were sick or wounded. Now she understood why the rebels were eager to become commanders. Chances of survival were greater and they could take as many wives as they wanted. Nobody cared about the ordinary recruits. Why should they? New abductees were constantly brought in from Uganda.

It was the fifth time her unit was going to loot a Dinka village, and it was becoming more and more difficult. The Dinka themselves were now starving and they had armed themselves to defend their scarce food stocks. During the first two attacks, she had been lucky and the villagers fled without offering any resistance. But the last two times, there had been heavy fighting and she was forced to use her gun. To her own surprise, Sarah found herself firing like an experienced soldier. There had been casualties on both sides.

They had to travel ever further to find some food. The village they were now heading for was two days' walk from the camp. A group of 150 rebels had been selected for the operation. Lakati was the over-all commander. He had been in Uganda for a few weeks and that had given Sarah some relief. At least she was able to sleep without fear of being called. She had to spend several nights in the trenches though, to keep guard. And in the absence of Lakati, the rebels often came to check if she wasn't sleeping with another man, or if her gun was properly tied to her body. When your gun was gone in the morning, you could expect a serious beating. And the penalty for adultery was death. Sarah recalled one love affair in the camp. When it was discovered, the boy and the girl were tied together and executed with one single bullet.

Her thoughts were interrupted by the sound of gunshots. The Dinka had obviously been informed of their coming and organised some resistance. In no time the village turned into a battlefield, guns rattling and mortars exploding. Sarah fired blindly. She had no idea whether she was hitting anybody. It didn't matter. It was about getting out alive now, about shooting or being shot.

When finally the last Dinka had fled and the dust settled, the village was littered with corpses. Some of her fellow rebels were lying among the dead and wounded. Sarah didn't take much notice of it. She had only one thought in her mind: food! She searched the huts and took as much sorghum as she could carry. But one could not cook sorghum without water, so she quickly ran over to the well. She placed the sorghum against a tree and started filling her jerrycan. Only then did she notice the Dinka soldier, standing only a few steps away, his gun pointed at her. At that very moment one of Kony's commanders snatched the bag of sorghum from under the tree. A shot rang out. The commander uttered a scream and collapsed. It was only a split second but enough for Sarah to get away. She heard a second shot. The bullet just missed her. Other rebels, who had followed her to the well, ran off too.

The journey back to the camp turned into a nightmare. Bad luck that she could not take any water, Sarah cursed as she pulled herself over the hot, arid land. She felt the blast of the hot sage-scented air on her face. It was as if the sun was slowly killing her, squeezing every bit of life out of her body. From time to time, she saw somebody drop down in the sand, not standing up again. Some asked their fellow rebels to urinate in a mug and then drank it. But Sarah couldn't bring herself to drink urine. Her throat was aching and burning, as if she was being strangled. She could hardly swallow or breathe. The next moment everything turned black before her eyes.

Night had fallen when Sarah regained consciousness. She looked around, astonished. She was buried in the sand up to her shoulders. Only her head rose above the soil. She tried to recall what had happened. She must have fainted. But how did she get into this pit? Suddenly it dawned on her. The rebels must have thought she was dead and must have buried her. She cried out for help, but there was a dead silence around her. The cool night breeze gave her new energy. She struggled to free herself, first clearing her hands, then pulling her body out of the sand.

Escaping back to Uganda was impossible, she thought. She was too weak and hungry to make it even to the border. So she just followed the rebels' track, a track marked by corpses. Dozens of corpses. The rest of the group was resting when she caught up with them. The first one to spot her stared at her with wide-open eyes. 'She has risen from the dead,' he screamed, terrified. But one of the girls burst out laughing. 'The sister must be praying very hard for her.'

Lakati didn't say anything. He was trying to get in touch with headquarters. 'We are dying! Send water!' he kept on repeating. At last, the cry for help was heard and a jerrycan of water was ferried to them. The commanders drank first. Lakati gave her some. It was the first time he ever showed any kind of care for her. But for those who had nobody to look after them, there was nothing left. They stayed behind as Sarah and the others stumbled to the camp.

18

*Like as ye have forsaken me, and served strange gods in your
land, so shall ye serve strangers in a land that is not yours.
(Jeremiah, 5)*

'The Aboke girls,' Museveni suddenly said. 'I want the Aboke girls
on the agenda.' His Sudanese colleague, Omar el Bashir, looked
surprised. He seemed not to know what his interlocutor was talking
about.

'All right, put the item on the agenda,' he nevertheless told the
mediator, President Daniel arap Moi of Kenya.

Rudolf Decker, a German national, looked inquiringly around the
table. Three African heads of state were assembled in all secrecy in
Eldoret, western Kenya. Three totally different personalities. There
was a lot they disagreed on. Yet there was one thing they had in
common: they were deeply religious. That was the basis for this 'prayer
breakfast' and all previous meetings that had been organised with
Decker's help.

The concept was first launched in the United States during the
Second World War. Parliamentarians and religious leaders came
together at regular intervals to pray, have breakfast together and talk
about problems in an informal way. US President Eisenhower met the
group and became a member. Since then, each American president
had attended the yearly prayer breakfast, the world's largest breakfast
with 3,000 guests. Decker, a successful engineer and a long-time
parliamentarian in Baden-Württemberg, was asked to introduce the
concept in Germany. With his colleagues, he formed a strong group
which also extended its activities to East Africa.

In that context, he had met the president of Sudan shortly after he
took power in 1989. Bashir had asked him to establish a link with
President Museveni in order to discuss the war in South Sudan. For
that was the essence of Decker's work: establishing links, making

connections, networking, like an engineer installing telephone lines. The content of the talks was something he got involved in as little as possible. The African leaders were best placed to find solutions to their problems, that was his philosophy.

Decker knew this meeting was crucial to the peace process in East Africa. It was meant to iron out differences between Sudan and Uganda before the Inter Governmental Authority on Drought and Development (IGADD) regional peace conference, which was to take place in Nairobi in three months' time. Tensions between both countries concentrated on the Sudan People's Liberation Army (SPLA). At previous meetings Bashir had accused Museveni of supporting the rebels in South Sudan, who were waging a long-time war against domination by the Islamic North. It was an open secret that Museveni sympathised with rebel leader John Garang and his struggle for the emancipation of the black man. As students at the University of Dar es Salaam, they had both been at the forefront of the struggle against Neo-Colonialism and for Pan-Africanism. But Decker knew there was more to it. Fearful of Islamic fundamentalism and accusing Sudan of supporting international terrorism, the US gave military help to Sudan's neighbours. Those neighbours, including Uganda, then passed on weapons to the Sudanese rebels. In retaliation, Sudan supported Ugandan rebel movements, one of them being the Lord's Resistance Army.

When the issue of the Aboke girls was raised, Bashir looked genuinely surprised by what Museveni told him. He shook his head. 'That Kony is a difficult man', he mumbled. He looked his Ugandan colleague in the eye and said firmly: 'Those practices are unacceptable to any sincere Muslim. If the girls are on my territory, you will get them back.'

***

With renewed hope Sister Rachele entered the office of Lars, a Scandinavian computer expert in Kampala. She had read in the newspaper that the Lord's Resistance Army had a website on the internet, and that it was possible to write to Kony. She had no idea what a website was or how she could send such a letter. But at least she had found a communication channel to Kony and she was determined to use it.

Lars was very helpful. He typed in the 'Lord's Resistance Army' and immediately found their website. With growing exasperation Sister Rachele read on the computer screen:

The Lord's Resistance Army is a national liberation movement, whose objectives are to liberate Uganda from tyranny, dictatorship, nepotism, oppression... We are fighting for the rights of all Ugandans, which the regime has denied them. That is why we enjoy the support of all the oppressed, right-thinking and alienated citizens of our country.

Lars browsed through the pages. 'They say they are committed to the cause of peace, democracy and human dignity,' he read out loud.

War and government instigated violence have been going on in various parts of Uganda. Worst hit areas have been the northern and eastern parts of the country where hundreds of thousands of people have been killed by the Museveni army. Thousands of orphans, widows, the disabled and the elderly are constantly being displaced from their homes and villages.

One of the last press releases predicted that Museveni's days were numbered.

We expect a major change on the ground in favour of the LRA and all oppressed Ugandans in the very near future, given the high morale and spirit of all the LRA commanders and fighters.

The web master was a certain Ben Otunnu in Columbia. Rachele looked at Lars, astonished. 'Can this be read all over the world?' she asked. He nodded. She shook her head in disbelief. The fact that Kony had a web site meant that the movement had intellectual and financial means. What seemed to be the most primitive of all guerrilla movements now appeared to be a modern organisation, with branches in London and the United States.

'Can I send a message to Joseph Kony?' she asked Lars.
He opened an empty page and she started dictating:

Dear Mr Joseph Kony,

Here is Sister Rachele from St Mary's College, Aboke, appealing to you. Please, be so kind and release our girls; they are the students of the college who were abducted by one of your commanders, Mr Mariano Ocaya-Lagira. Twenty four of our girls are still with you.

She gave their names and ended with: 'Thank you very much. May God bless you.'

The answer from Otunnu didn't take long.

I have in the past expressed my concern by asking the LRA High Command to expedite the investigation of this matter and to immediately release these girls if they are holding them or any other persons being held against their will. I will once again reiterate the urgency of this matter and emphasize that this kind of behaviour does not help to reach their goals.

He expressed his sincere regret for 'the hardship this matter has caused' to Sister Rachele and the parents, and ended:

I will contact their headquarters to inquire as to the where-abouts of the girls. Expect me to e-mail you early next week.

But Otunnu was not heard of again. Time and again it had been like that, Sister Rachele reflected as she undertook the four-hour journey back to Aboke. Each time she felt she had made a breakthrough and had found a way to get to Kony, the communication abruptly stopped and the path died out. But her mind was firmly made up. She would go to Kony's camps in Sudan and get the girls herself, with or without connections.

19

I came near to death; I was on the brink of the grave. They
surrounded me on every side, and there was no one to help me.
(Ecclesiasticus 51, 6-7)

Sarah rushed to the prayer ground. Kony had called an assembly. There
was tension in the air. She sensed it from the nervous way the
commanders had been running about all morning. 'The Holy Spirit
has spoken to me,' Kony began as usual. Lakwena had told him that
700 Ugandan soldiers had crossed into Sudan. They had linked up
with the SPLA, and the united forces were advancing towards the camp.
Sarah knew the information didn't come from Lakwena but from the
rebel groups in northern Uganda, who were in touch with the
headquarters by radio. Two hundred and fifty rebels were selected to
go and fight the force. The rest had to be on stand-by.

Sarah returned to her family and went about her normal household
duties: preparing food, cutting grass to build huts and cultivating
potatoes and vegetables. She couldn't really be bothered. In fact, she
didn't care whether she was alive or dead, whether she died of hunger
or was killed by a bullet. If only this madness would end.

As time went by and there was no news from the rebels, fear in the
camp mounted. Reinforcements were sent to the front, a second group
of 120 rebels. At last some fighters returned from the battlefield, defeated
and wounded. They talked of great losses. Panic struck. First the Sudanese
soldiers in the adjoining camp took off. They left on foot or on the back
of lorries. Then Kony fled. 'We will take refuge near Juba and return
later to defeat them,' he said before he boarded his car.

His pick-up had just disappeared from sight when there was a terrible
explosion. A mortar had hit one of the trucks. Then, with a thunderous
noise, tanks came rolling in from the other side. The rebels all started
running. Sarah stood nailed to the ground, staring at the tanks that
crushed the first huts on the outskirts of the camp as if they were

cardboard boxes. She couldn't make herself move. After all, the attackers weren't really her enemies.

She sat down against a big tree, watching the scenes around her with dazed eyes. Most of the rebels had now fled. Only Juma Oris' men stayed behind to keep up the resistance. They fought from trenches, trying to stop the advancing troops with heavy mortar fire. Everywhere, bombs were exploding, huts burning, and the dead accumulating. 'It is better to die,' she told herself. 'Where should I go anyway? My country is Uganda, but here I am far away in Sudan.'

The Oris rebels called on her to join them. 'I cannot fight,' she shouted back. 'I'm hungry.' For hours she remained sitting under the tree, watching the battle rage on. Until dusk fell and the last of the Oris men fled. Suddenly, an awkward silence descended upon the smoking remains of the camp, only interrupted by the groaning of the wounded. Realising that she had survived the worst of all battles, Sarah felt a spark of hope flaring up inside. As if she woke up from a long sleep.

'You wanted to die,' she said loudly to herself. 'But maybe this is your day to go home.'

She got up, tied her luggage and saucepan on her back, took her gun and carefully made her way through dozens of bodies. There were little ones too, she noticed, even some of the children born in the camp. She had taken only a few steps when a bullet whizzed close behind her. The saucepan on her back was smashed to the ground. She thought she had been hit and dropped down. But nothing happened. Realising she was unharmed, she got up again and took only the gun and the magazines. 'If something happens to you, you must throw away everything and only keep your weapon,' somebody had once advised her. 'Because when the rebels find you without a weapon, they will think you are trying to escape.' As long as she had the gun she could say that she got lost.

On the other hand, moving around armed also carried a risk. She could be taken for a rebel and be killed by the other side. But the enemy, she concluded, was not the Ugandan army or the SPLA. The enemy was not the Dinka population which they had attacked and killed and looted. The real enemy was Kony's movement that had kept her prisoner for six months. The real enemy was the Sudanese army that could bring her back to Kony. All alone she walked over the barren land of South Sudan. The stars were her only friends. She didn't know where she was, nor where she was heading for. She only knew she had to keep on moving westwards from Juba. From her Geography lessons she knew that it was in the direction of Zaire.

The night turned into day, and the day into night again. Still she was wandering over the endless ruined plains, without meeting a living soul or coming across any form of habitation. She didn't dare sleep, for fear of being eaten by leopards, and she lived on mud from the river.

On the morning of the third day, she suddenly saw figures emerging on the skyline. As they came closer, she saw they were rebels, two boys and eight girls. They all had guns. There were no commanders.

'Where are you going?' they asked her.

Her mind was working fast. 'I'm going to Uganda.' She pointed in the direction of Juba: 'There's heavy fighting over there. A lot of our people have fled to Uganda. Let's go and join them there.'

The rebels looked at her suspiciously. 'We have to follow Kony', the oldest boy exclaimed.

'Who are you anyway?' one of the girls intervened. 'Are you not one of those Aboke girls?'

'We should shut her up with a bullet,' the boy shouted.

She looked him straight in the eye. 'Shoot me. I'm not afraid of dying. Do it!'

Her defiance seemed to intrigue the girls. 'Maybe she's right', one of them threw in. 'Maybe we should follow her.'

The others hesitated. Finally, one by one, they took her side. Only the boys refused. 'We cannot follow a girl,' they said, setting off in the direction of Juba.

Sarah could sense the mistrust of the girls as they followed her. They advanced slowly. Everybody was weakened by hunger. Sarah felt her head go light again and her throat being squeezed. She was relieved when they came across a river. They all fell on their knees, gulping down handfuls of water and stuffing their mouths with mud. Sarah slowly felt her strength returning. 'We have to cross the river,' she told the others.

'It's too deep,' the girls declined.' Or do you want us to drown?' Again they threatened to kill her.

'Spare your bullets. I'll get drowned', she screamed back, stepping fearlessly into the river. Rather by accident she found a shallow place and waded to the other side. The others stared at her in astonishment. Then they took off their slippers and followed her track.

'If we want to survive, we have to throw away our guns now,' Sarah said when everybody had reached the other bank. 'Otherwise we will be killed by the Dinka.'

The girls protested fiercely. Now they were convinced she was plotting to have them killed. Another quarrel ensued. And once more, Sarah managed to convince them. They hid their guns in a small thorn bush and continued walking. From a distance, Sarah spotted a homestead. From the way the huts were built she could tell it was a Dinka homestead. Naked children were playing outside. She called them but as soon as they saw her, they ran into the huts. The next moment the Dinka ran out and hid themselves in the bush behind. Some had guns. It was obvious that they were waiting for them.

'We have to flee,' her fellow rebels urged.

Sarah couldn't believe her own calm. 'When we flee, these people will shoot us,' she heard herself say. 'It is time to surrender. If we die, it's fine. It's God's will.' The girls started laughing. 'You are completely mad!'

Sarah peered at them, her eyes threatening. 'If you run, I'm going to scream that you are the ones who abducted me, so that they only kill you.' Her threat was effective. Reluctantly, they followed her. Sarah now walked with her hands up towards the Dinka homestead. 'We are not bad people,' she shouted in English. 'We were kidnapped from Uganda. Some of us were taken from their schools.' The other girls too started shouting, each in her own language. When they were standing right in front of the homestead, the Dinka people slowly emerged. The men came first, their guns at the ready. They searched them to be sure they were not armed. Communication appeared to be impossible: their languages were mutually incomprehensible. Sarah saw the Dinka gesticulating and waving their fingers angrily at them. She figured out that the Dinka blamed them for attacking their villages and stealing their food. Their hands were tied and the girls were paraded before the Dinka men, who positioned themselves in front of them like a firing squad.

Sarah looked daringly into the barrels. 'You are going to kill us, but we are not bad people,' she shouted continuously. 'We were abducted from Uganda. Some of us were taken from school. We have come to you for help!' She was the only one in the group who spoke English. Her fellow rebels had no words anymore. They were trembling all over.

Suddenly, an old man emerged from the back of the homestead, holding a panga. He stopped right in front of Sarah, scrutinising her. She was convinced he was going to hack her to pieces. He motioned the men to wait and then turned back to her. 'What did you say?' he asked in broken English. She repeated her words and he said something to the men. They slowly put down their guns and squatted down under a tree, where a discussion erupted. The girls were untied and invited by the old man to sit down. Porridge and water were served and they wolfed down the food like starving people. Then the old man informed them he was going to take them to the nearest SPLA camp. The commander there would have to decide what to do with them.

It was a strange caravan that set itself in motion, the old Dinka man followed by nine destitute Ugandan girls. On the way, they met a group of Dinka soldiers and a fierce argument flared up. Sarah sensed that the soldiers were blaming the old man for rescuing them.

'They want to kill you,' he explained. 'They say you're useless.'

And what had he answered? He smiled. 'I told them that I am a Christian and that they cannot kill you in front of me. It is up to the commander to decide about your fate.'

Sarah didn't know what to expect from the SPLA commander. Surely, he was not going to have mercy on them after all those attacks by the Kony rebels on their positions.

Arriving at the SPLA camp, they were taken straight to the commander's hut. The man who was to decide whether they would live or die was a huge black fellow with scars on his face. Sarah was glad he spoke English. At least she could explain to him who they were. She told him about the abduction, the journey to Sudan, the forced fighting and the attack on Aru, which gave them the chance to escape. In the end, she begged him to take them home. He grunted from time to time, listening without looking at her. Then he turned to the old man. Sarah could feel that the *Mzee* defended their case fiercely. At last the commander looked at her, his face more friendly now. 'All right, you can stay here. We'll see what we can do.'

He gave an order to his subordonates and they returned with some food. Sarah was surprised. Here they were in an SPLA camp, braving the lion in his den, and they were not only kept alive but even looked after. For Sarah, the commander was too kind to be trusted.

They were assigned to a hut and the waiting started. As the days passed and nothing happened, Sarah's anxiety grew. Not that there was any cause for fear. The Dinka soldiers kept at a respectful distance from them, only bringing them food. Nobody was guarding them either. Where would they go anyway? Sarah had no idea where in South Sudan they were.

'We'll take you to the border,' the commander announced one morning.

They were driven on the back of a pick-up to yet another SPLA camp. Are they fooling us? Sarah wondered. Was this another trick? They were introduced to a commander called John Garang. He was even bigger and darker than the first one, but he was equally friendly. He offered them a cup of tea and announced in perfect English that he would take them to General Salim Saleh. Sarah got frightened. Had Salim Saleh not been killed? At least that's what Kony had told them. 'But first we'll take you to Aru,' Garang smiled. They were loaded onto the pick-up again and driven over the barren land back to the camp. But there was not much left of Aru. The place where Sarah had spent the worst four months of her life, was razed to the ground. Corpses were still lying about, in an advanced stage of decomposition. The commander showed them pictures of Kony that had been recovered from the ashes.

Then they were driven to another military base and introduced to General Salim Saleh. When Sarah saw the man, she was convinced that it was a trap. This light-skinned man couldn't possibly be Salim Saleh. He looked rather like an Arab.

'Where do you come from?' he questioned her.

She was so confused that she could not utter a word. He looked at her with interest.

'Are you from Aboke?'

She wanted to deny it. After all the mention of Aboke had already caused her so much trouble, but she could only nod. Suddenly, a smile appeared on his face.

'Then you are the ones we were looking for. Get yourself ready. I will take you to Uganda.'

20

And if thine hand offend thee, cut it off... and if thine foot offend
thee, cut it off... and if thine eye offend thee, pluck it out.
(St Mark 9, 43, 45, 47)

George Omona watched the open truck drive into the reception centre
at Gulu. Its load consisted of children: 190 children. They were
offloaded in front of a crowd of spectators who stretched out to look at
them. Some had come to see what the rebels, who had attacked their
villages and killed their relatives, looked like. But others, George knew,
had come in the vague hope that maybe their son or daughter had
come home.

More than 2,000 children had escaped from the Lord's Resistance
Army in the last two years. Because the first reception centre – run by
World Vision – could hardly handle the influx, George had now opened
a second one, called Gusco. How many more? he wondered. How
many more of these broken little souls would he need to collect, nourish
and very carefully heal so that they could return to society more or
less in one piece?

There were not only the visible wounds: the swollen feet, the scars
of bullets and cuts, the mutilations, the skin diseases and germ
infections, the malnutrition which had sometimes hampered their
growth and development, the back pains from carrying heavy loads,
the venereal diseases and pregnancies. Worse, and more difficult to
heal, were the inner scars: the fear and mistrust, the feelings of guilt
and self-contempt, and the anger towards a society that had failed to
protect them.

George sighed. What a heavy price for misplaced pride, for clinging
to lost glory! As an Acholi, George knew the background of the conflict
better than anyone. He was the deputy headmaster of a secondary school
when Museveni took power in 1986. He recalled the propaganda spread
by the defeated Acholi soldiers: Museveni's troops would come and

take revenge on the Acholi people for the killings in the Luwero Triangle. Even a respected elder of George's village had called upon the youngsters to take up arms to defend Gulu. After all, many people had benefited in one way or another from the Luwero cleansing. If only because looted goods had been sent to the north. So the population had sided with the rebels, for fear of being punished.

George's main criticism of the rebels was that they had never given Museveni a chance. The Acholi soldiers believed that they were unbeatable, that they could not be ruled by another force, and that power belonged to them. When finally an Acholi had climbed to the highest position, he was chased out by Museveni only weeks after both had signed a peace agreement on power sharing. George knew his countrymen felt cheated. 'We paved the way for Museveni by overthrowing Obote, and Museveni paid us back by betraying us,' they woud say. But then again, he argued, Okello's government was the most shameful of all. It took months to form a cabinet, which was constantly being reshuffled, and he never managed to have control over the entire capital, let alone the entire country.

The appearance of Alice Lakwena had given the Acholi cause a new boost. Many of George's friends believed she was a saint who gave the demoralised Acholi back their pride. Under her military and spiritual guidance, the resistance against Museveni turned into a popular rebellion. She not only commanded a battalion of soldiers, she also wanted to cleanse the Acholi of the evil spirits which, in her view, were the cause of their misery. Alleged witches were killed, or abducted and purified with shea nut oil. Violence was justified in the struggle to bring the Acholi people back on the right track. Once the rebellion had started, the government forces also committed excesses. While initially Museveni's army had been an example of discipline, this changed briefly when a unit from the Luwero Triange was sent to the north to fight the rebellion.

But it was mainly the disappearance of the cattle which gave the Acholi an alibi to continue the war. George knew that his fellow men blamed the government for the loss of their cattle. To them, it was the ultimate proof of Museveni's strategy to wipe out the people of the north. For the cows were everything to the Acholi: they were the basic source of their diet, they were used as draught-animals to cultivate the fields, they served as dowry and were used for the settlement of disputes.

Deep inside, however, George knew that everybody participated in the cattle raids. He had seen Acholi soldiers and Lakwena's forces confiscate animals, which they promised to repay later, after they had overthrown the government. Museveni's troops also stole cattle to support their operations. And the Karimojong from the east, notorious cattle raiders, took advantage of the power vacuum to penetrate deep into Acholi land and take their share. They had acquired arms from Amin's troops on the run from Uganda, and later from the government to defend themselves against cattle raiding by the Turkana from neighbouring Kenya.

Those Acholi who had lost the most cattle were today Kony's last supporters. For the majority of the population had long turned their back on the rebels. When Lakwena's troops were defeated, most former soldiers accepted Museveni's offer of amnesty and joined the new national army. Only a hard core did not trust it and continued the fight.

Frustrated over the lack of support from their own people, they started recruiting by force and punishing 'traitors'. George recalled one morning in 1994 when, on his way to school, he found 15 bodies on the side of the road, their heads smashed. It was just after the collapse of the peace talks and the Ugandan authorities had called upon the population to stand up against the rebels. People had to arm themselves with axes and spears and to raise the alarm whenever the rebels were sighted. Kony's answer did not leave much room to the imagination. The lips that would betray them were cut off, the ears that would hear their secrets were slashed off and the eyes that could see them were gouged out.

At the same time Sudan started arming Kony. The alleged negotiations between Kony and the government of Sudan were the main reason for Museveni to break off the talks with the rebels and give them a seven-day ultimatum to lay down their arms. Kony's terror drove the people even further into the arms of the government. In their hundreds of thousands, they fled to the cities or to protected camps located around military posts.

Then the first abducted children came home. George saw them arrive at his school, showing up out of nowhere after a long absence. They behaved strangely, struggled with discipline and complained of being attacked by the spirits of the people they had killed. It had been George's first real confrontation with the madness of the Lord's Resistance Army and it hadn't left him since.

He looked at the miserable wrecks with their restless looks and battered bodies lining up on the ground in front of him. He knew that these children were the key to 'enter' into Kony's mind. Their stories could help him to complete the puzzle and try to make some sense out of this terrible suffering.

***

Deeply touched, Norman listened to the speeches at the reception centre in Gulu. They were many, all escaped children like himself.

'We are happy to welcome you here today,' the director said. 'We accept you back as our children. Whatever you have done, you were forced to do it. It was not your fault.'

The words went straight to Norman's heart. He had spent weeks in the military barracks, feeling like a criminal. Sometimes, they didn't get food all day. At night, his fellow prisoners screamed out their nightmares and Norman had been afraid that the spirits of the dead would also haunt him.

The trip to the reception centre on the back of the lorry had been particularly terrible. People had been staring at them with hostile eyes and the guards had warned them that if they lost their balance, they would fall onto their bayonets.

'The community that could not protect you, now turns against you and calls you rebels,' the director continued. 'But you were forced. You are not bad children. We still love you.'

The boy next to Norman jokingly pinched him in the arm. When he turned round, he looked into the twinkling eyes of Stephen. The boy was younger than Norman and had been with the rebels only a few months. But he was nice and understanding. Norman instantly felt that he had found a friend, someone he could trust and talk to. And for the first time in two years, he smiled, a roguish, boyish smile.

They were given new clothes and sent for a shower. Norman let the water run over his body for a long time, as if to get rid of all the dirt from the bush. Then he lined up for lunch. Stephen was standing next to him when a *muzungu* man took a picture of them. He wondered who this old man was.

His happiness was complete when his parents came to see him later. They couldn't believe it, they said. A boy, who had been abducted together with him but escaped earlier, had told them that their son was dead. Norman was glad that they didn't ask him to come home. They were prepared to move to another village, they said, so that the rebels would never find him again. But he didn't trust it. He wanted to stay in the centre as long as possible. Here he felt at home and safe, among all those boys and girls who understood and forgave him without his having to explain anything, the ones he had abducted and the ones who had abducted him, the ones he had beaten and the ones who had beaten him, and those whose relatives he had been forced to kill. At night, when they were all lying in the dark side by side, Norman knew that he was protected from the spirits of the dead, that they could not reach him anymore.

***

Sarah stared blankly into the distance. She was sitting in front of General Salim Saleh's hut at the military headquarters in Gulu, wearing her best dress. Next to her was Justine, who had escaped about the same time as she had. Justine was out fetching water when the Aru camp was attacked. Instead of fleeing to Juba, she had run towards the camp and hidden in one of the trenches, until she was buried by sand and dust and everybody thought she was dead. When she got up the next morning, she bumped into a Ugandan soldier who asked her if she was from Aboke, after which she was taken to Uganda.

Sarah's father was sitting in the front row, next to Sister Rachele and Justine's mother. The white visitor was seated in the middle. He had come all the way from Germany to listen to their story. But Sarah couldn't talk or concentrate on anything. Even the homecoming hadn't been as happy as she had expected. Of course, her father and her friend Ellen had been overjoyed, and the sister had cried. But her thoughts kept drifting off to a world she could not explain. However much she tried, she could not find the words for all the scenes she had so meticulously stored away. It was as if a glass wall separated her from the rest of the world. She was constantly frightened, and she noticed that others were frightened of her too. They looked at her strangely when she was sitting on her own, staring into the distance, or when she ran outside and let the rain run on her face for four minutes.

The meeting started. She was relieved that she did not have to say much. Justine was doing most of the talking. Her friend told the group about the forced killings, the fighting, the marching, the hunger and thirst. But then she broke down in tears and could not go on. Sarah noticed she had skipped the worst part. That part they had only told the colonel's wife, whom they were staying with. With her they could talk about their humiliations and pain and fears. And about that shameful disease they had brought along. Salim Saleh had encouraged them to put their memories on paper. Sarah had spent several days writing a diary. And this diary she now handed to this foreigner who had come all the way from Germany.

21

*I have spread out my hands all the day unto a rebellious peo-
ple, which walketh in a way that is not good, after their own
thoughts... A people which eat swine's flesh. (Isaiah 65, 2-4)*

It was a sunny Sunday morning in June when a military jeep drove up
the dirt track to St Mary's School. Mass had just ended and the army
vehicle was a source of great interest to the churchgoers. Sister Rachele
came running out of the dining room, surprised to see the intelligence
officer. She invited him in but he declined.

'Sister, there's a possibility you can go to Sudan and visit Kony's
camp to identify your girls. Ben Pere can accompany you.'

He paused for a while, clearly pleased to bring her the good news
in person.

'Be ready,' he added. 'Tomorrow, I'll come and collect you.'

Sister Rachele turned to her superior in disbelief. 'Alba, I'm going
to Sudan,' she shouted with joy. 'I'm going to get the girls!'

She immediately left for Lira to inform Ben. The prospect of going
to collect his daughters filled the man with emotions too strong for
words. Then he turned practical. They should get pictures of the missing
girls, he said. They should also prepare a list with the names of the
commanders to whom they were allotted. His face changed as he wrote
down the name of Vincent Otti, his comrade in Obote's army, who
had taken his daughter Jacqueline as his wife. But he quickly composed
himself and got on with the preparations.

On their way to Kampala the following morning, they were
wondering how all this had come about. Or would the German man
have something to do with it? They had met Decker over a month ago
in Gulu. It had not been clear to Sister Rachele what his mandate was.
All she knew was that he was a personal friend of both the presidents
of Sudan and Uganda, and that he was trying to make them resolve
their differences. Whatever his role or mandate, he had been another

source of hope for Sister Rachele. For if the conflict between both countries was resolved, she reasoned, the children would come home.

It was a large delegation that boarded a Kenya Airways flight to Nairobi a few days later. Apart from Sister Rachele, there was her superior, Ben, as chairman of the Concerned Parents Association and three officials of the Ugandan intelligence service, including the intelligence officer of Gulu and David Pulkol, the overall chief of Uganda External Security Organisation. Pulkol had given them the details of the mission. They would travel to the LRA camps in South Sudan to identify the girls. Arrangements for the visit had been made at the highest level, between the two presidents. Uganda would pay for the travel expenses, Sudan would bear the cost of accommodation and transport in Sudan.

This could not go wrong, Sister Rachele thought as she considered the elaborate preparations. At Nairobi airport, where they had to wait for their connecting flight, a messenger from the Sudanese embassy came to inform them that their visas would be ready on arrival. Even the Uganda high commissioner passed by to wish them luck. At last they boarded the plane and took off, destined for Khartoum.

'This is like a dream,' Sister Rachele thought as they flew over South Sudan. She clasped her bag, containing the pictures of the 21 missing girls, and a list with the names of the commanders which they had drawn up with the help of Sarah and Justine.

Her thoughts went back to that morning in April when a military helicopter came to collect her from the school. 'I have both good and bad news,' the colonel in Gulu told her. 'The good news is that Justine was rescued. The bad news is that she was the only Aboke girl we found in Aru camp.' Justine was the first girl to come back from Sudan and her stories had upset Sister Rachele so much that she couldn't sleep for nights. A week later, when nobody was expecting it, Sarah suddenly turned up. She was found together with eight other girls who were so grateful to her that they called her 'mummy.' And halfway through May, Pamela came back, with a shrapnel in her nose. Pamela had been given to a commander in Uganda but was rejected because she was 'too small.'

The 'fasten your seat belts' sign in the aircraft was switched on. Sister Rachele looked out of the window. Khartoum was covered in darkness. She didn't know much about this country, except that there had been a war for almost half a century between the government in Khartoum, mainly representing the Islamic North, and rebel groups representing the African and Christian people of the South. She also knew that since the 1989 coup, the country had adopted radical Islamic policies and all democratic institutions had been abolished. Islamic law - or *Sharia* - had been introduced, the constitution suspended, the independent press closed down, political parties and trade unions dissolved and all non-religious organisations banned. A network of Islamic security services was said to control all areas of public life.

With screeching brakes the plane came to a halt. As soon as Sister Rachele came through the door, the hot humid air blew into her face, as if she was walking into an oven. A security man was waiting for them. He led them to the VIP lounge, where a government representative in a long white dress and a white turban welcomed them and helped them with their visas. Because it was late, they were taken to their hotels immediately. The two sisters, Ben and the Gulu security officer were lodged in the Hotel Meridien in Khartoum Central; Pulkol and the other security agent in the Hotel Palace in Khartoum North.

***

Rudolf Decker was just about to finish a book on his mediation attempts in Rwanda when the phone rang. It was Abubakar, President Bashir's political adviser.

'Could you come to Khartoum right away? We need you to bring the case of the abducted children to a successful end.'

'What happened?' Decker inquired.

'You will remember that President Museveni requested us to release the schoolgirls during our meeting in Eldoret. Well then, at the summit of the Organisation of African Unity last month, the two presidents decided that a Ugandan delegation could travel to Sudan to secure the release of the girls. The Ugandans have now arrived. They include the

115

two sisters of the school, the chairman of the parents' association and the head of the Ugandan security.'

Decker paused for a while. Of course, he remembered. He had even met two of the Aboke girls during his visit to Gulu and he had been deeply shocked by their story. He also recalled his own promise. If he could be of any use in this humanitarian operation, he would not hesitate to come to Sudan.

'Tomorrow there is a Lufthansa flight to Khartoum,' he said. 'I'll try and get a seat.'

That was more easily said than done. The plane appeared to be fully booked. Only after a series of persistent phone calls did Decker manage to get a seat for himself and his son. In the afternoon another obstacle arose. He had been feeling miserable all day, but now he could no longer ignore the signs of a bad cold. In the evening he even got a temperature. Could he travel in this condition? His thoughts went to the sisters who were waiting in Khartoum. He knew the Sudanese would not undertake anything without him.

'If I manage to get up in the morning, we'll go,' he told his son before going to bed, burning with fever.

***

Sister Rachele stared out over the waters of the Nile. The little breeze was a welcome relief from the intense heat of the city. They had been invited to a boat-lunch by Dr Gutbi, chief of the Sudanese intelligence service and Pulkol's counterpart. The food was delicious and the atmosphere relaxed.

'Our government takes securing the release of the Aboke girls very seriously,' their host assured them. 'To us, Muslims, this is a moral and religious matter. We would not like to mix it up with political issues.' He promised his full cooperation and predicted that their visit would be very productive and successful.

Sister Rachele leaned back reassured. For three days, they had been in Khartoum and she was getting a little worried. There wasn't much to do except wait and wonder what they were waiting for. Once they were taken on a sight-seeing trip across the city, but Sister Rachele couldn't concentrate on anything but the mission they had come for. This clear and firm assurance gave her new hope.

But her optimism vanished when they got back to the hotel later in the afternoon. Pulkol handed her a report of the Ugandan intelligence service. With growing exasperation, Rachele read about the preparations Kony and his commanders had made in anticipation of their visit: all weapons and uniforms in the camps had to be removed, unnecessary movement to be stopped and no communication to take place between the Sudanese army and the LRA. Important decisions should wait until Kony returned from Khartoum. The Aboke girls would be transferred to another camp, which the visitors would not get to see. The Sudanese leadership in Juba or in the camps should not be informed about these preparations, it emphasised. 'Otherwise they might be instructed by their superiors in Khartoum to search the camps for the girls.' And the intelligence report concluded: 'The visit is being stage-managed by the LRA into a window dressing exercise.'

Sister Rachele felt her courage sink with every word.

'What are you going to do with this?' she finally asked Pulkol.

'We are meeting President Bashir tomorrow. I will give him a copy of the report and insist on having a high-ranking Sudanese officer accompany us to the camps. This officer should have sufficient power and authority to direct the commanders in the south to make surprise checks on all the camps. Without such guarantees, we should not be leaving.'

She sipped her tea, which tasted remarkably sweet. Suddenly, she remembered where she had drunk such tea before: at the camp with Lagira before leaving the thirty girls behind. If only she could talk to that commander again. She was convinced there was some goodness in that man. Had he not voluntarily given her that small girl to take home?

Early the next morning they were collected and taken to the president's office. Bashir, a sturdy man dressed in a military uniform, welcomed them warmly. He repeated what Dr Gutbi had already told them: that the abduction of the girls was a matter of moral concern to him and to his government, and that he would do his utmost to ensure their release. 'I have already issued an order to the field commanders in the south to co-operate fully with the delegation,' he said.

Sister Rachele studied his face as Pulkol handed him the Ugandan intelligence report while outlining the main points and summarising the recommendations. But Bashir didn't blink. He assured them again of his government's total commitment to the release of the Aboke girls and promised to send a team headed by Faizal, a security man from his office.

'You are free to go wherever you want and search any camp,' he emphasized. 'However, Juba being a war zone, the Ugandan security men will not be able to join the team to the south.' It was that last remark in particularly that worried Sister Rachele.

Before leaving, a picture was taken of the entire group. The Comboni sisters, who were the smallest and stood in front, stared with an anxious look into the camera. In the back row, towering over the rest, were the Ugandans. Bashir, the sturdy officer in whom they had put all their hopes, was standing in the middle, smiling.

22

*They come from a far country from the end of heaven, even the
Lord, and the weapons of his indignation, to destroy the whole
land. (Isaiah 13, 5)*

The wind howled and whistled around the military wing of Khartoum
airport. It was the time of the *haboobs*, the notorious desert winds
which sweep up the sand to whirling columns and at times impenetrable
curtains of dust. It was five o'clock in the morning. Decker wiped the
sleep and the sand from his eyes. He found it difficult to get used to
the short nights that seemed to be part of his African journeys. He had
not yet recovered from his cold and had enjoyed less than three hours
of sleep. Due to the sandstorm, his Lufthansa flight had been delayed
for many hours. Abubakar and the minister responsible for state security
had been waiting for him at the airport. Only to tell him that the flight
to Juba was to leave at half past four in the morning. To Decker's
astonishment, he had found the entire Ugandan delegation waiting for
him in the hotel lobby, despite the fact that it was very late. He had
noticed the relief on the faces of the Italian sisters and he knew, there
and then, that he had taken the right decision.

There was no sign of activity at the airport. The hours passed. Faizal,
their escort from the president's office, stayed discreetly in the
background. It was a characteristic which Decker generally appreciated,
but this time he wished their guide would be a bit more active in finding
out what was happening.

Finally, they were taken back to their hotels. The flight was cancelled
for today, Faizal simply announced. '*Bukra insha-allah*' - tomorrow,
God willing. There was no time to catch up on sleep however. Decker
wanted to take advantage of the extra day to try and meet rebel leader
Joseph Kony who, according to his sources, was staying in Khartoum.
He requested Faizal to try to fix an appointment. The waiting also
gave him the opportunity to accept the ambassador's invitation to lunch.

A remarkable group had assembled at the residence of the German ambassador. There were the French ambassador, the editors of two opposition newspapers and a prominent government official responsible for human rights. Not surprisingly, the subject of the conversation was the latest peace deal in Sudan of April 1997. Although the main faction of the SPLA had refused to sign it, Decker considered it an important step towards ending Africa's longest war. The peace treaty no longer excluded the possibility of secession for the south. During the only period of peace Sudan had known since independence, the south also enjoyed some kind of autonomy. But when in 1983 the region was re-divided and brought back under the rule of Khartoum, the war flared up again.

A war about religion: the Islamic-Arabic north versus the Christian-African south. But the war was even more about the country's natural resources: water and oil. The digging of the Jonglei-canal, channelling more water from the Nile tributaries to the north, and the construction of a pipeline to pump the oil to the northern port of Port Sudan, were considered by the southerners as attempts to take their resources away.

Since the war resumed in 1983, already more than one million people had lost their lives: killed by hunger and disease, killed in the fighting between the government army and the SPLA, or - less well-known - between the different factions of the SPLA.

In Sudan, like in Uganda, the root causes of the conflict went back to British colonial rule, which had left the south largely underdeveloped. The Arabs, who had been ruling Sudan ever since independence, in turn did nothing to develop the south. Worse, they considered their black countrymen as inferior people – slaves. A form of *apartheid* had been established in Sudan in the last half century. Human rights organisations spoke of a deliberate policy of extermination of the south.

Not all northerners seemed to be happy with the latest peace plan, Decker discovered during the discussion. 'Treason,' his interlocutors called it. 'In this way, you cut off the country's feet.' Although Decker did not entirely agree, he found it surprising that such open criticism of the government was possible. It confirmed what he had been suspecting for some time: that the climate in Sudan was changing.

It was almost midnight when he heard from Faizal again. 'I have spoken to Kony,' he said in a conspiratorial way. 'He apologises that a meeting is not possible for now. He is not feeling well, but he wants to see us on our return from the south.'

'And the appointment for tomorrow is still valid?'

'Yes, you will be collected at five o'clock.

***

Sister Rachele fiddled with her veil. The waiting was making her nervous. She wished they would be up and gone already. A second intelligence report that Pulkol showed her just before their departure, had upset her. The rebels had changed their plans and the girls were now going to be relocated to the front line, in the hope that the visitors would not go there. Had somebody leaked the first report? Rachele wondered. New directives had been issued to the camps too: all the wounded had to be evacuated from the women's camp. Only some mothers with children could stay behind, but they were not allowed to speak to the visitors. Commander Margaret was the only one to answer their questions. The report strongly recommended that the Sudanese government should now seriously discuss the release of the Aboke girls with Kony in Khartoum. And it ended with the warning: 'Since Uganda is committed to the idea of releasing the Sudanese prisoners of war immediately after receiving the 21 girls, the failure of the current operation will definitely slow down progress on political and diplomatic issues.'

Rachele took a deep breath and looked at the others. It was unfortunate that Pulkol and the Ugandan security men had to stay behind in Khartoum. But at least Decker was there. His presence, and the cooperation of the German embassy, gave the mission a more official character. She had overheard the German ambassador offering a charter plane to ferry the girls back.

In the pale light of the morning, she saw a column of soldiers marching towards them. They took positions in a huge square, so that one line nearly reached the place where their group was standing. Most soldiers wore sandals and carried their few belongings in a plastic bag.

'Soldiers of the rebel faction that signed the peace treaty,' Ben whispered. 'They are now sent to the front to fight against their own brothers. What a shame for Africa!'

Faizal judged that this was not an appropriate waiting place for the visitors and guided them to the VIP lounge, where they were immediately collected again and taken to a Boeing converted into a cargo plane. An endless line of soldiers disappeared into the tail of the plane, all clasping their plastic bags. In the end, the aircraft was so full that there was no place left for the delegation.

'Next one,' Faizal shrugged as he herded them back to the VIP lounge.

By eleven o'clock another equally old Boeing was being loaded with what looked like sacks of wheat. A new line of soldiers filled the belly of the aircraft. Faizal announced proudly that he had managed to obtain two seats in the passenger cabin. Decker offered them to the sisters but Rachele resolutely declined. Decker and his son had to sit in front, she insisted. She herself climbed on top of the sacks in the back, where the heat and the smell were almost unbearable.

***

Decker had to admit that he didn't feel entirely comfortable about this mission. Only now did he realise that none of his high-placed contacts in Khartoum was accompanying them. He had only met Faizal a day earlier, though from the respectful way the man was being saluted at the airport, he concluded that he must be high in rank. In the war zone in the south, they would be cut off from the outside world. There were no telephone lines and they would not have a radio transmitter at their disposal. Moreover, air traffic was completely unreliable, dependent on the weather conditions and on rebel activity. Decker had repeatedly asked his friends in Khartoum whether the necessary safety provisions would be in place. Protection had been arranged, he was assured. They would be in the care of the Sudanese commanders in the south.

But his first concern now was the plane that was supposed to take them to Juba. The safety belts were broken and through the open cockpit door, Decker saw the flight engineer work the switches on the instrument panel with his fist. The temperature was rising to intolerable levels. The steward offered them a plastic cup of water, scooped from a bucket under their feet, and he seemed surprised that his passengers declined.

'This plane is very old,' the captain apologised when they were invited into the cockpit after take-off. 'But this little box contains the most modern electronic navigation system.'

'Is it a risky flight?' Decker carefully inquired.

'Only the last bit, just before the landing in Juba. The rebels have SAM-7 missiles that can reach up to 4,000 metres. We have to fly at maximum height above Juba and then go down in a kind of nose dive.' He smiled when he saw Decker frown. 'Don't forget that we do this every day. And look, we are still alive!'

After a couple of hours, Juba appeared beneath them. Decker and his son were nervously watching the preparations for landing. The captain was talking in Arabic over the radio. 'I was just asked if you were on board,' he turned to them. 'They had been expecting you in the morning.'

The plane hovered above the city for a while. Then it set off for the steep descent. Decker had never gone down so quickly. It was with relief that he felt the plane touch the ground. He thanked the captain and his crew and climbed out, wondering what other adventures were awaiting them.

23

*Destruction cometh, and they shall seek peace and there shall
be none. Mischief shall come upon mischief, and rumour shall
be upon rumour. (Ezekiel 7, 25-26)*

Sister Rachele was glad to be rescued from the dark, sticky belly of
the plane. The smell had been terrible and the noise had made any
conversation impossible. She was also relieved to see that a military
escort was waiting for them. Faizal introduced them to a Sudanese
colonel and to Hassan, a man in civilian clothes who appeared to be
the chief of security in Juba.

'Welcome to Juba,' the colonel greeted them. 'We were expecting
you earlier.'

They were led to three jeeps, in which soldiers with machine guns
were posted in the back. Juba was clearly a city in decline, Sister
Rachele noticed as they drove into the city centre. If this collection of
ruins and destroyed houses was worthy of that name, that is. The roads
were full of potholes, some as big as craters. A sign at the central
roundabout pointed to the former Belgian Congo. Time must indeed
have stopped then in this part of the world.

It struck her that the place was green, greener than she had imagined
from the stories of the children. But then, this was the rainy season.
And the camp where Sarah and Justine had been held was quite a
distance from Juba, closer to the Ugandan border. Since Aru had been
overrun, the rebels had moved their base. From Pulkol's report, Sister
Rachele could make out that there were three camps now: one at Mile
15 called Nisitu women's camp, a second at Mile 34 where Kony's
headquarters were, and a third at the front line at Mile 39, opposite the
first SPLA camp which was at Mile 40.

They were taken to Hotel 'El Salam,' the only one in the city. The
rooms were not ready yet and they had to wait in the lobby, where
some soldiers were staring at a screaming television screen. There

wasn't any time to inspect the rooms as they were told to proceed to the camps immediately. The delegation was divided among the three jeeps. Sister Rachele and her superior were in the car with Hassan. Ben Pere was seated with Faizal, and the two Germans joined the colonel.

Soon they were out of the city and on to the Juba-Gulu road. It was not so much a road as a rough, bumpy and heavily rutted track. Sister Rachele carefully registered the surrounding landscape. This was certainly the most desolate place she had ever seen. There were no tarmac roads, no stone buildings, no cultivated fields, no cars and... no people. Sporadically, some huts with cone-shaped roofs emerged, but these seemed to be inhabited by soldiers only. Soldiers were the only human beings they met all the way. Soldiers guarded the small iron bridge over the Nile. Soldiers patrolled the dirt track and manned the roadblocks that were thrown up every other mile.

At Mile 15 they stopped at a Sudanese army checkpoint. In the bush some distance from the road was the LRA camp for pregnant women and mothers with babies, their escorts explained. 'Maybe we could go and have a look there first.' They left the cars behind and proceeded on foot through the low bush. Reaching the assembly of huts, Sister Rachele immediately noticed that the place was deserted, except for a few elderly men. The women were out collecting firewood, they said. The colonel ordered them to fetch the inhabitants. In the meantime Sister Rachele and her superior set about searching the huts. But they were all empty.

After a couple of minutes, the first women emerged from the bush. Some were pregnant, others carried small children on their backs or at their breasts. All in all, about 50 women turned up. They got seated on the ground and looked at the visitors with hostile eyes.

'Have you seen the Aboke girls?' Sister Rachele asked. 'Do you know where they are?'

'Go away,' the women screamed back. 'Why did you come here? This is a refugee camp!' And then, in chorus: 'You killed our relatives in Uganda and we fled here because of Museveni's government. Now you have followed us again to kill us here.'

'Girls...,' Sister Rachele tried to calm them. But the screaming continued.

'We are refugees in Sudan. We came here a long time ago. We never want to go back to Uganda!'

The sister looked at them bewildered. There was something unreal about the situation, as if the women were performing a well-prepared act. Suddenly, she remembered the Ugandan intelligence report. When a woman in her 30s started addressing them, she turned to her.

'Are you Margaret?'

There was a moment of confusion. The Sudanese motioned to her to go away. With Margaret out of the way, Sister Rachele hoped the women would talk more freely.

'Please, tell me if our girls are here,' she pleaded.

But the women just stared at her, their lips were sealed. However hard she insisted, they wouldn't say another word.

'If this is a registered refugee camp,' Decker intervened, 'then show us the refugee list and the food distribution manifest.'

'This is an LRA camp, not a refugee camp,' the Sudanese colonel asserted.

'Where are the other women then? There are fewer people here than the size of the settlement indicates.'

'Maybe we should wait for the others to return from collecting firewood,' the colonel suggested. 'After all, it is getting late. I don't think we should proceed to the other camps, since that is a war zone. We can visit those tomorrow.'

Rachele looked up. 'We have the president's permission to search all the camps,' she said sharply. 'We know our girls are there.'

'Yes, let's proceed to the other camps,' Faizal supported her. The colonel conceded, though reluctantly, and they walked back to the jeeps.

They drove in silence for a while. Sister Rachele peered out of the window. 'If we find one Aboke girl, we'll find them all', one of the Sudanese had said. 'Then we have proof of their existence.' Oh, how she wished she could catch a glimpse of one of them! She clasped her bag, which contained the list and the pictures. She knew she would recognise them immediately, whatever condition they were in.

They reached Mile 34, Kony's headquarters. But there was no living soul there.

'This is an old abandoned camp,' Hassan told them as they passed. They stopped at a Sudanese army camp which lay right behind it, and discussed whether or not to proceed.

'Everything is quiet at the front,' the colonel judged.

'Then we go,' Decker decided.

As they arrived at Mile 39, a series of shots were fired in the air. Getting out, Sister Rachele immediately noticed that a Sudanese army camp bordered that of the LRA. In fact, they ran into each other, only a stick at the side of the road marked the separation. It was obvious: Kony's camp was a buffer between the fighting parties in Sudan. Only one mile away was the first SPLA line.

In no time, they were surrounded by four soldiers who stared at them with grim looks on their faces. They wore military uniforms without stripes and carried modern machine guns and walkie-talkies.

'Can we talk to your commander?' the colonel asked one of them.

But the man shook his head. 'They are far away and are not coming.'

Hassan explained that this was a directive from President Bashir for the team to collect the Aboke girls.

The man shrugged. 'I don't know anything about the Aboke girls.'

After a while, a commander emerged from the bush. Ben could hardly hide his emotions. He greeted the man in Langi and called him by name. Sister Rachele immediately knew what was going on. 'Are you Otti Vincent?' she asked. He nodded.

She showed the colonel his name on the list.

'According to our information, one of the Aboke girls is in your possession,' the colonel said, showing him the picture of Ben's daughter. But the man denied the allegation fiercely.

'He claims he doesn't have the girl,' the colonel said to Sister Rachele.

She looked the LRA commander straight in the eye and said slowly and sharply: 'I was told that in April he had the girl.'

The man turned away, not commenting.

'Are there any women here?' the colonel said in an attempt to break the impasse.

'There are,' he reluctantly admitted. 'But they have nothing to do with the ones you are looking for.' He paused for a while and then added: 'Supposedly those were here.'

'Could we see them?'

The commander issued an order to the other rebels. While they were waiting, Decker tried to start a conversation with the rebel leader.

'My name is Rudolf. And who are you?'

'I am Vincent.'

'We want to help to end this war and to find a peaceful solution,' Decker continued.

'I also want peace. We all do.'

'Then you can make a significant contribution. If these girls should be found, it would be an important step towards peace. I beg for your cooperation. Please, help us!'

The man searched for an appropriate answer. 'I am like a trained dog,' he then said. 'When I am sent somewhere, I'll go. When I am called back, I come back. Do you understand that?'

Decker nodded. He realised that further questions were useless. This was a soldier who simply followed orders.

From the bush, groups of three to four female fighters emerged. Most were barefooted, dressed in skirts and blouses and carrying heavy weapons on their shoulders. About 50 girls in total took position in three lines in front of the visitors. The youngest looked about 14, the oldest hardly 18. There was fear and anguish in their eyes.

Slaves, Sister Rachele could not find a better word to describe them. These were slaves, children brutally abused, living in daily fear for their lives. She could hardly control her tears. Ben was weeping too. The colonel asked them to undertake an identification exercise. As she moved closer, she tried to talk to them in Lango.

'What is your name?'

No reply.

'Where do you come from?'

Silence.

The menace from the rebels around them was pervasive. One wrong word, she knew, and these girls would not live long after they were gone.

'May I pray with them?' she finally asked the commander. He agreed.

'Our Father who art in Heaven...,' she started in Langi.

'Hallowed be Thy Name...,' the girls joined in Acholi.

Ever louder grew the choir of misery.

'Thy Kingdom come. Thy will be done...'

Decker could not bear it any longer. Tears welled up in his eyes.

'And deliver us from evil. Amen.'

Dozens of eyes followed them as they walked back to their vehicles and drove off. The night was rapidly folding around them and the atmosphere at the road blocks had grown more grim. At every post, two soldiers stopped the convoy, their guns at the ready. The Sudanese colonel in the first car then shouted something to a third soldier, who flashed a torch at them before they were allowed to pass.

None of this was noticed by Sister Rachele. Her mind was utterly confused. She felt overcome by the same emotions of powerlessness and despair as when she left the thirty girls behind eight months earlier. Faizal tried to comfort her.

'I know a few houses in Juba which are regularly visited by Kony's soldiers. Maybe we could check there,' he proposed. 'After all, the matter must be settled today, because tomorrow morning you are flying back.'

Everybody agreed and they proceeded to a suburb of Juba which was engulfed in darkness. The cars halted in front of a wrought iron gate. They got out and entered into a yard which contained several scattered huts. Sleeping figures were lying about. It took some time before they found someone responsible for the place. And when they did, the guard refused all cooperation.

'The president himself has ordered this mission,' Hassan insisted. 'This is an action of the Sudanese government!' But his words made no impression on the boy. Faizal took him aside, trying to persuade him. In the meantime, Sister Rachele and her superior had found a sick boy in one of the huts who claimed he had heard of the Aboke girls. But however much they pressed him, he would not say more.

At last Faizal managed to persuade the guard to guide them to a compound where girls were being kept. The camp was in another suburb called Gumbo. When they arrived at the place, they indeed found some girls outside in the courtyard, eating their supper. Some looked even younger than the ones they had seen at the front line. Sister Rachele greeted them in Lango but nobody greeted her back. It was strange for Africans not to greet, she reflected.

'Do you know where the Aboke girls are?'

Again they ran up against a wall of silence.

'Where do you come from?'

A girl let slip that she was from Moyo, but she was instantly silenced by one of the male inhabitants.

Tired, hungry and totally demoralised, the delegation returned to the hotel. At night the dimly lit place looked even more depressing, and - as Decker remarked - more dangerous. He wondered if their safety was assured. They discussed the day's events, especially the mysterious 'old abandoned camp' at Mile 34. Ben claimed he had seen laundry hanging out to dry, chickens running about and fresh footprints in the mud.

'What about making a surprise visit to that camp early in the morning?' one of the Sudanese suddenly suggested. 'We won't inform anyone, not even our soldiers.'

The sisters and Ben immediately agreed. Decker was sceptical but he didn't want to seem an obstacle. 'If there is just a glimmer of hope of finding the girls, all other considerations must be put aside,' he said, getting up to retire to his room. The others followed suit. Tomorrow would be another early day.

24

But they that escape of them shall escape, and shall be on the mountains like doves of the valleys, all of them mourning, every one for his iniquity. (Ezekiel 7, 16)

They left Juba before dawn. It was drizzling and the road had now turned into a mud path. The going was slow and required careful manoeuvering through the deep tracks. Again they passed the iron bridge, Nisitu camp and the numerous road blocks. Even the first light of the day could not dispel the gloomy atmosphere that hung over the desolate landscape.

It was almost seven when they approached Mile 34. At a glance, Sister Rachele saw that the camp was now teeming with life. Their arrival created commotion and panic. Children were running in all directions. They disappeared into the huts or the nearby bushes. Sister Rachele thought she saw one of her girls, a figure with a cooking pan on her head. She quickly jumped out of the car and ran towards the camp. But one of the rebels, a teenage boy, stopped them and invited them to sit down.

'We have not come to sit. We have come to collect the Aboke girls,' Hassan replied.

The boy gave him a furious look. 'How dare you talk to me like that!'

His brutality towards the security chief of Juba shocked Rachele.

'Please, I am the sister from Aboke. I am the one to whom Lagira gave some of the girls back. Help me to find the others.'

The rebel's face relaxed a bit. 'If you put it like that, we can talk.'

Hassan explained the aim of their visit and the boy finally agreed that they search the camp. Ben had already disappeared into one of the huts. Suddenly he came out, pulling three girls along. 'These children say that our girls are here,' he shouted in excitement. 'They were not allowed to tell us, but I've promised that we would take them with us to Uganda if they talked to us.'

131

A strained silence followed. Decker stared at Ben, shocked. The girls looked down, their attitude revealing deadly fear. The Sudanese colonel came forward. Slowly, emphasising each word, he said to Ben: 'How dare you make such a promise!'

Ben turned to the sisters in dismay. 'But their lives are in danger,' he stammered. 'We can take them with us, can't we?'

'Not only these girls are in danger,' Sister Rachele said firmly. 'All the children here are in danger.'

The atmosphere turned hostile. Several rebels were now pressing around them, jeering at Ben and waving a finger accusingly at the girls. Decker tried to save the situation. He consulted with the Sudanese, but they asserted that their assignment concerned the 21 Aboke girls only.

'Let me take a picture of these girls,' the German finally said. 'I am sure nothing will happen to them.'

Sister Rachele noticed that some rebels had walked to the other side of the road. In an act of despair she ran over to them, showing them the pictures of the Aboke girls.

'Is Lagira here?' she begged. 'He gave me the 109 girls. Please, let me talk to him. I am sure he will hand over the others too.'

Decker cut her short. 'Sister, come, we have to go.'

There was something in his voice that stopped her asking any further questions. They hastily returned to the vehicles. Nobody dared look back at the three girls who stayed behind.

***

Decker was in deep thought all the way back to Juba. What a terrible mistake Ben had made, he thought. He hoped and prayed that the three girls would be all right. At the same time he realised this was the desperate act of a man who knew his missing daughters were nearby. What an unbearable situation for a father!

He sighed. He was convinced their own lives had been in danger too. He had clearly sensed the hostility in the air. Without the Sudanese they would probably not have come out alive.

He tried to analyse the situation. The Aboke girls were only the tip of the iceberg. Thousands of others were being abused and exposed to constant danger. The girls had the advantage and at the same time the disadvantage that they had become famous, because of the actions of Sister Rachele and the parents' association. But that was not making their situation any easier. After all they had been given to some of the top commanders. Their release would be perceived as a serious blow to the movement and lower the morale of the commanders.

The role of Sudan, it now occurred to him, was much more complex than he had thought. He had seen how the boy treated the security chief of Juba. And how the rebels were keeping the frontline east of Juba. The question was: Who needed who most? Only peace could bring an end to this tragedy, he concluded. And in that peace process, Museveni and Bashir were the key players. The IGADD meeting could not fail.

But Decker's first and foremost concern was now getting out of Juba fast. Staying much longer would not be advisable. He particularly feared for the safety of the sister and Ben.

Bad news was awaiting them at the hotel. The plane had not yet arrived. Nobody knew whether it would still be coming. For security reasons, Decker requested a visit to the Juba military headquarters. After all, his contacts in Khartoum had promised him protection by the commanders in Juba. To his surprise, they were immediately invited to *fatur*, the late Muslim breakfast.

***

Sister Rachele was heart-broken. She hardly noticed what was being said during the meal at the military barracks in Juba. Their delegation was sitting at one table, and the Sudanese officers at another table. Over and over again, Ben related his conversation with the girls in the hut. The Aboke girls had been hidden in the bush the previous day, they had told him. It was like the intelligence report had predicted: everything had been a set-up.

After breakfast, they were received by the chief of staff in a separate room. Decker informed the general about their findings. Sister Rachele handed him the names and pictures of the missing girls. The general looked at the pictures and promised to send one of his colonels back to the camps and continue searching.

'All along, the LRA have made us believe that the women and children in the camps were their relatives,' the man explained.

Sister Rachele shook her head. 'Most are abducted children,' she asserted. 'They live in the camps under terror and against their will.'

'The abduction of women and children is a common occurrence in war,' the general replied. 'Even the SPLA have recently abducted some children.' Then he leaned forward and said in a low voice. 'Suppose the girls were found and refused to go back to Uganda. Suppose they want to stay with their husbands.' He glanced at Ben. 'Even the father here says that they can stay if they want, as long as compensation is paid.'

Ben wanted to object but Rachele silenced him.

'Let me talk to my girls,' she said sharply. 'None of these girls would want to stay here!'

The general turned to Decker.

'Why is Museveni putting so much emphasis on these Aboke girls, when there are more important issues to discuss?' he asked. 'Why does Uganda not seek to bring Kony into the peace process and ask the release of all the children?'

Sister Rachele did not hear Decker's reply. She was seething with indignation. How could Ben have said such a thing?

She put the question to him as soon as they left the headquarters.

'But I didn't say that!' he objected. 'They have twisted my words!'

One of the Sudanese had earlier suggested to him that the girls might want to stay with their husbands. 'They are not married, because no dowry has been paid,' Ben had replied.

It struck Sister Rachele that a careless remark by Ben had immediately been picked up and used as an excuse. The message seemed to be: 'OK, we have found the girls. But they don't want to come. They prefer to stay with their husbands.'

134

They spent the rest of the day idly on the hotel terrace. Their morale was down. Nobody felt like talking much. The Sudanese hosts had all disappeared. There was no car or taxi, and no sight of their guards. Only in the evening did Faizal appear again, to tell them what they already knew: that the day's flight had been cancelled. *'Bukra insha'alla.'* And they should not worry about their safety, he assured Decker. 'You are being guarded all the time.'

It was not until the following afternoon that an old Boeing nose-dived into Juba. The off-loading and loading was done in record time and the pilot started the engines even before all the passengers had climbed in. Tears rolled down Rachele's face as they took off. We have to leave them behind, it ran through her mind. We know they are there and yet we have to leave them behind.

25

Thy people is scattered upon the mountains, and no man gathereth them. There is no healing of thy bruise; thy wound is grievous. (Nahum 3, 18-19)

'I am told that the problem of the girls has been solved. Can you come back to Sudan?'

Decker couldn't suppress a sigh. He had just returned to Germany and was still trying to come to terms with the failure of the last visit. And now this phone call again from the president's office.

'Where are they then?' he asked Abubakar.

'We will talk about that in Khartoum.'

'Do we have to go back to the south?'

'That too will be discussed when you're here. Can you make sure the sisters are coming as well?'

The German pondered for a while. The vagueness surrounding this new visit made him reluctant. But having started this mission, should they not do everything to bring it to a successful conclusion? The IGADD conference was only one week away. He knew Museveni had made the release of the girls as a condition for his participation. After all, the Aboke case threatened to tarnish his country's image. The donors were becoming involved. And investors were being scared off. Unwittingly, the Aboke girls had become the key to the peace process in the region: the queens in East Africa's political chess game.

'All right, I'll take the next Luftansa flight,' he replied.

***

Once again, Sister Rachele and her superior were waiting in the transit lounge at Nairobi airport. The flight to Khartoum was delayed for many hours, giving them plenty of time to assess these new developments. 'The job is done,' was the message they had received from the office of the Ugandan president. Sister Rachele knew Museveni had now thrown his full weight behind the effort to get the girls released. 'Bashir lost a golden opportunity', he had commented when they reported to State House after their return from Sudan. 'If he had released the Aboke girls, I would have reopened the Ugandan embassy in Khartoum tomorrow.'

Not much of these high level discussions was reflected on the ground, however. The situation in northern Uganda was as bad as ever, with rebel attacks occurring almost on daily basis. The newest tactics seemed to be the ambushing of vehicles, spurring everyone who still ventured up the Gulu-Kitgum road to drive in convoys, protected by military escorts. But even that could not deter the rebels. In Kitgum alone, seven such convoys had been attacked in the past two weeks; dozens of passengers had been killed or wounded.

It was past midnight when the plane finally set off for Sudan, and dawn was breaking when they landed once more in the *haboob*-stricken Sudanese capital. The sisters were collected from the airport and driven straight to the Hilton Hotel, where Decker was waiting for them. A strange group of people had assembled in his room. Hassan was there and Dr Mutrif, the Sudanese deputy chief of intelligence, and three Ugandan men in dark suits whom Sister Rachele had never seen before. The greeting was formal. Decker expressed his satisfaction with the meeting and asked the guests to introduce themselves. One of the Ugandans presented himself as Major Dominique Wanyama, the general secretary of the Lord's Resistance Army. Sister Rachele recognised the name immediately. This was the spokesman she had tried in vain to get in touch with in Nairobi. The second Ugandan introduced himself as Major Sam Ochola, the LRA secretary for defence, and the third as Livingstone Opiro, the chief of logistics and engineering. Their mistrust was obvious. Decker's proposal to have something to eat in the room was resolutely rejected. Not even a drink was accepted.

Then Wanyama took the floor. 'I am here to represent the movement and its chairman,' he said. 'As I had promised to the head of the Red Cross, I did some research to locate these girls. They are with us.

Their abduction was the act of an unruly commander.' He paused and looked around. For Sister Rachele this was an important step. For the first time, the Lord's Resistance Army admitted they had the girls.

'But they never left Uganda,' he went on. 'They are scattered in the four districts of northern Uganda. What we are asking is a temporary cease-fire for the girls to be collected and handed over to the sister.' He turned to her. 'I believe she has a radio. The date and place of the hand-over will be communicated to her by radio. There should be no government operations during the entire period of the ceasefire. If our soldiers are seen moving with the girls, no action should be undertaken.'

Rachele's superior intervened. 'The radio is granted to us only for common communication, not for other purposes,' she threw in. 'I must apply to the Italian embassy for the exceptional use of the radio to this end.'

'Maybe the Red Cross frequency could be used,' Dr Mutrif suggested.

'During the hand-over, no representative of the Ugandan government is to be present,' Wanyama continued undisturbed. 'Only the sisters, Decker, two or three Sudanese witnesses and a delegate of the International Committee of the Red Cross can be there.'

'How long will the entire process take?' Decker wanted to know.

'The operation of moving the girls could begin in two or three days from now. The entire operation could take one or two weeks. We need an answer in writing from Museveni himself.'

'Which form should the answer take? Would a fax do?' Decker asked.

'A fax or through the media. But a written form is needed and it must be from Museveni.' Decker got up and retreated to the adjoining room to try and contact Museveni's office.

'If the ceasefire is immediate, five days should do,' Hassan commented.

'No, we can't act that quickly.'

'A week is enough!' the Sudanese insisted.

The sisters returned to the issue of radio communication. They agreed that a frequency would be sought. The time of communication was set at 11 am, and code names were agreed upon.

After a while Decker came back, a frown on his face. 'Uganda needs more time to consult,' he announced. 'An answer will not be expected until later today.'

He sat down and turned to Wanyama.

'Would you be ready to have peace talks with Museveni? Bashir is very interested to broker this peace. It would be good if the matter could be solved before the IGADD conference next week.'

'We are not in Museveni's time-table!' Wanyama replied sharply. 'When Museveni will be ready, it will be up to our council to decide who will represent us in dealing with him.'

Dr Mutrif invited the sisters to the adjoining room but they declined, eager to hear the rest of the discussion.

'Let it be clear that we are only responding to international calls, not to Museveni's,' Wanyama continued. 'Museveni will never solve the problem. He will never win!'

Major Livingstone, who had not said a word, made an abrupt end to the conversation. 'We have three issues here that should not be mixed up. First, there is the case of the girls. Secondly, there is the regional conflict and IGADD. And thirdly, there is the political dialogue with Uganda. We are only here to deal with the girls.'

They stood up. 'Our mission has come to an end here,' Wanyama concluded. 'We don't need to meet each other again.'

Decker spent most of the afternoon on the phone with Pulkol, the Ugandan chief of external security. Both knew that their telephone conversations were being tapped. But they had nothing to hide. Decker felt great hesitation on the other side.

'The rebels are militarily weak at the moment. They could use a two week ceasefire to strengthen their positions in northern Uganda and bring more arms in,' Pulkol objected.

'But the girls would be free then,' Decker suggested.

'Who says so? We are not even sure of that. We relied on a promise like that during the 1994 peace talks. It took us months to recover from that mistake, and many soldiers lost their lives. Besides, nothing came out of it.' Pulkol faced yet another problem, of a constitutional nature. The decision on a ceasefire could not be taken without the consent of the Ugandan parliament. But the parliamentarians were only discussing a proposal for amnesty.

***

Sister Rachele was already back in Uganda when she learnt about the outcome of the talks. She and her superior had taken the first flight back to Uganda because their presence was no longer required. Decker would handle the rest of the case.

'We have given them three options,' Museveni said on their return to Kampala. 'First, we don't consider their proposal. Second, we consider it but we don't accept it. Third, we accept it but on our conditions. We will determine the place and date for the release. The place will be cordoned off. Only the sister goes forward, the girls are handed over to her and she comes back with the girls.'

Sister Rachele agreed to this. She had contacted the parents and they had raised a strong objection to the ceasefire. It would give the rebels the chance to enter Uganda in great numbers, which would endanger thousands of other children in the north. Nobody wanted to take responsibility for such a scenario. After all, the girls were not even in Uganda. Why was all this time needed to collect them?

A few days later, Kony's spokesperson issued a press release. The LRA's proposal for the release of the Aboke girls had been rejected by the Ugandan government, it said. 'What happens to the girls from now on is no longer our responsibility.'

The IGADD conference in Nairobi came to nothing. President Museveni did not show up. Only a few insiders knew the real reason for his absence.

26

And they shall be as mighty men, which tread down their enemies in the mire of the streets in the battle; and they shall fight, because the Lord is with them. (Zechariah 10, 5)

George stared out over the courtyard of Gusco. There was a worried expression on his face. Very few children had escaped in the past months. There had been a steady flow of children coming to his centre in May and June 1997. But then, all of a sudden, it stopped. The months of July and August were understandably quiet because the rebels had retreated to Sudan. But a large group had invaded again at the end of August. Kony himself was said to have crossed the border with 300 men. Since then, there had been fighting almost every day. The army claimed they had rescued and captured more than 500 rebels in recent months. But it was now well into November and where, for God's sake, were they?

George suspected the army was keeping the children in the barracks, so as to get a constant flow of information from them. Some said the children were being used as scouts to point out the rebels' hidden arms depots. To the parents, their children were being abducted a second time. George had raised the matter with the local authorities but they were reluctant to take action. They had no authority over the army, they claimed. The relations between the local politicians and the military were strained as the army suspected them of supporting the LRA.

So in the end, George had turned to Unicef for help. The country representative had considered the matter serious enough to fly over from Kampala and talk to the commanders. She had found the cells full of children. Some had been there for three months. It had taken a great deal of effort to convince the military authorities that these were not rebels but abducted children, and that they should not be in barracks but in reception centres.

And today, finally, the children would be released. With his colleague of World Vision, George had arranged to send buses to the military headquarters in the morning to ferry the children to the reception centres. But the bus drivers had been turned away without any explanation. More worrying, the radio had been calling upon the population to attend the event. To George, that was a bad sign. He recalled one incident the previous year when children were handed over to an angry crowd to be lynched.

He stared at the courtyard where some escapees were re-enacting their abduction, as part of their therapy. Carrying bundles of straw like guns under their arms, they stormed into an imaginary homestead, dragged out the 'children' and beat anyone who resisted. The others watched with their eyes wide open. Nobody laughed at the clumsily enacted scenes or the mock beatings. Among the spectators was Francis, a nine-year-old boy who had been forced to kill a woman while she was holding her baby. Next to him was ten-year-old Daniel, who had been forced to watch the rebels kill his mother. In a corner, all on his own, sat James. He had been abducted at the age of 18 and made a commander right away. His task had been to abduct children and shoot those who ran away. In all, he had killed 120 people. Every time he felt eager to kill again, he retired into a corner on his own, desperately trying to keep himself under control.

George took a deep breath. For months, he had been listening to stories that made his blood chill. There were no limits to the rebels' sadism and cruelty. All means were used to dehumanise these children. Some had been forced to hack their parents to death with an axe in the presence of other relatives. Others had to stab their school's headmaster and then sit on the body, or dip their hands in the victim's blood and eat with blood on their hands. George sometimes felt so sick that he just wanted to walk out and never come back. But then he saw the children recovering in a few months' time, like faded flowers that, given some water, care and love, started blooming again, and he felt almost ashamed about his moments of depression.

But it was hard! The first group of children to arrive in Gusco were so suspicious that they refused to eat the food they were given. George had to wash his hands with them and eat from the same plate to prove that there was no poison. Then he had given them new clothes and made them burn their military uniform. A symbolic act: a sign that they had broken with the past and begun a new life. He would never forget the looks in their eyes when they stared into that fire.

Then the most difficult part started: to win their confidence, get them to speak, even about the unspeakable. It was like helping them throw up the things they could not digest and which prevented them from functioning. Some children had not talked since their return, as if they had been struck dumb. Others were plagued by epileptic fits, throwing themselves on the floor and shaking violently. Many complained of nightmares, even during day time. For hours, George would sit in the grass next to a child struggling to come to terms with the guilt and shame, not looking up at him, playing compulsively with his sandals. Those who could not express themselves acted out their past in role plays, they drew pictures or used music as an outlet, singing, playing instruments or dancing themselves into a trance.

George encouraged them to play with the children of the nearby village, so as to lower the barriers with society and make them feel part of it again. Though he knew that he had to keep a close eye on such games. Once, a discussion that flared up during a soccer match turned into a fight!

He looked at his watch. It was coming to four. In less than three hours it would be dark. He decided to go and check at the military headquarters what was happening. He had just reached the post office when he saw them: a long line of destitute children. Some of them had torn clothes, some were displaying gunshot wounds. Most were malnourished. They walked barefoot through the town centre, in the rain, while spectators on both sides of the road were jeering and shouting insults at them. George impulsively joined the line. For the first time, he experienced what the children were going through. The onlookers, mainly refugees from the surrounding villages, took him for a rebel leader and called him a killer. As the soldiers paraded them around the market place, George hardly dared look up. The journey over the muddy road to the Gusco reception centre seemed to last forever. When they finally reached the gate, he burst into tears. But he quickly composed himself. There was no time to lose. It was getting dark and there was no electricity.

He made them sit under some plastic sheeting, to protect them from the rain, and started registering them. There were 287 children in all. Those from outside Gulu were sent to World Vision. A hundred and thirty stayed with George. They were served high protein cookies and porridge

'This is not of your making,' George kept telling the children who sat huddled together like a herd of threatened sheep. 'We accept you as children but we do not approve of the things you were forced to do. Consider this to be a resting place, a kind of hospital. As soon as you feel better, you can go home.'

Night had fallen. It was too dark for a shower, so the children were sent straight to bed. Only then did George realise that he did not have enough trunk beds. He filled up his office and the corridors with mattresses. He did not want to leave them alone. So after having made sure everybody had found a place to sleep, he stretched himself out between them on the floor. The smell was unbearable. But worse even were the sounds: the crying and groaning of the wounded, the coughing and laboured breathing of those with tuberculosis and chest infections, the raving of those with fever, and now and the screaming of those who woke up from nightmares. His greatest fear was that some would not survive the night. There was nothing he could do at this hour, nothing but walk from room to room, sit next to them holding their hands, and hope that this long and terrible night would finally come to an end.

27

There are others who are unremembered, they are dead, and it is as though they had never existed, as though they had never been born. (Ecclesiasticus 44, 9)

Once more, Sister Rachele, Ben and Angelina were making the two-hour journey to Gulu. The mood in the car was gloomy, everybody consumed by their own thoughts. The article in the *New Vision* had created panic. 'Kony executes five girls by firing squad,' the headline read. One, reportedly, was a girl of Aboke. As no names were mentioned, all the parents were deeply perturbed. So Sister Rachele decided to go and check the story for herself. She had heard that a large group of escapees had arrived at the reception centres in Gulu. Surely, somebody must be able to confirm the killing and provide them with more details.

There had been a lot of developments since their return from Sudan six months ago. Together with Ben, she had been part of Museveni's delegation at the Sudan-Uganda peace talks in South Africa, initiated by President Nelson Mandela. They had waited all day outside the conference room in Pretoria for the outcome of the talks. But during the press conference afterwards, little leaked out. Mandela only asserted that 'progress' had been made, but he declined to give any details.

'Have the Aboke girls been discussed?' a journalist asked.

'That too must remain in the realm of confidentiality,' Museveni had replied.

At the end, Sister Rachele had shaken hands with Mandela and President Mugabe of Zimbabwe. She had also met Bashir again and he had embraced her.

Their visit to Sudan had apparently caused a disruption within the ranks of the Lord's Resistance Army. A month after their return, Alfred Banya, Kony's representative in London, announced he had been sacked because he wanted the Aboke girls and others 'held against

145

their will' to be freed. 'It became clear that the new political godfathers of the LRA, who are based in London and elsewhere, are positively engaged in hindering the release of the Aboke girls,' he stated in a press release. The rebels reacted by claiming that they never raided the school at Aboke. They had only 'rescued' the girls from the front line and were keeping them in 'safe custody', the new spokesman in Nairobi, Dr Obita, said in an interview with the BBC. The parents had been furious, not in the least because the BBC had spread such blatant lies. 'Since Obita has accepted responsibility for the whereabouts of our children, we are requesting him to release them soon. If not, we shall take him to the international courts of law,' they replied in a written statement.

The first anniversary of the abduction had been marked by a prayer ceremony at Lira stadium and a full-page advertisement in all the newspapers, displaying the names of hundreds of missing children, including those of the 21 Aboke girls. Thousands of students had taken to the streets of Kampala in the biggest protest march against the war ever, urging the government to talk peace with the rebels. 'Release the Aboke girls,' their banners read, and 'If you can't kill Kony, talk to him.' Kony reacted a few days later. 'We will not talk peace with terrorists like Museveni, who is a murderer and a liar,' he stated in a press release. 'We will only talk on the battlefield. This war will never end unless Museveni is defeated and brought to trial for the atrocities he has committed.'

At about the same time, Unicef announced that at least 12,000 children had been abducted in the north over the past five years, 70 percent aged between 12 and 15. Half of those abducted were feared dead. The Children's Fund also explained why fewer girls than boys escaped. 'Girls are made wives of commanders and are always near the camps, giving them fewer chances of escaping.' And Unicef came to the disturbing conclusion: 'A third of the country's children who go to bed are not sure they will wake up safely.'

At the end of that month, President Museveni surprised friend and enemy by announcing that he would accept an amnesty for the rebels. 'I am under strong pressure,' he said on his return from the Commonwealth summit. 'Because of the numerous crimes they have committed, I have never supported negotiating with this particular group. But I have agreed to an amnesty. They will not be prosecuted for the crimes they have committed.' Asked if the amnesty also referred to Kony and his top commanders, he said: 'I will consider whether we can include the whole gang.'

These were little sparks of hope, enough for Sister Rachele and the parents to keep going. But then Jacqueline's mother had passed away. The worry about her daughter had become too much for her, being a single mother and Jaccqueline being her only child.

And now there was this article in the paper...

They turned into the Gusco reception centre, where George gave them a warm welcome. It was the first time for Sister Rachele to meet the Gusco director. She immediately felt they were of the same mind, as if they were companions on this bizarre trip into Kony's underworld. Ben explained the purpose of their visit and George immediately selected some of the new arrivals and assisted in the tiresome interrogations. It was about Jenny, the headgirl to whom Sister Rachele had given her rosary. With some other girls, Jenny had been accused of getting on too well with the Arabs, because they had accepted some extra food. Kony in person had ordered their killing. But then contradictions entered into the story. Some claimed the girls were shot. Others said they were beaten to death. None of the children they interviewed had actually witnessed the killing. It left Sister Rachele and the parents with a glimmer of hope. They decided to tape the testimonies and analyse them later, in the presence of Jenny's father.

'I remember the sister,' one of the girls they interrogated suddenly said. 'She came to the camp in Sudan.'

Sister Rachele looked up in surprise.

'Where were you then?'

'I was among the group at the front line.'

'The group with whom I prayed?'

The girl nodded. Sister Rachele embraced her, tears in her eyes.

'Why didn't you talk to us?'

'We were ordered not to say anything, to pretend we didn't understand Acholi. Otherwise, we would be killed after you were gone.'

'Where were our girls at that moment?' Ben asked.

'They were there in the bush. All of them.'

'And the gunshots, what did that mean?'

'That was the signal to announce your arrival so that the children could go and hide.'

A boy remembered them too. He was at Mile 34 - the headquarters - that morning when they made their surprise visit.

'They wanted to kill you,' he said.

'But we were accompanied by Sudanese officers,' Rachele threw in.

'That's why they did not do it.'

'What happened to the three girls who talked to us?' Ben inquired. Rachele knew the question had been on his mind ever since they had returned from Sudan.

'One of them, a girl called Monica, was killed after your departure.'

Ben's face turned grim.

'Shot?'

'No, the noise would have alarmed you. They broke her neck with an iron bar.'

The news hit Ben hard.

'Are you sure?' Sister Rachele insisted.

'Yes, I was one of the four boys who buried her.'

There was a long silence. Ben suddenly looked years older. Sister Rachele knew he felt personally responsible. She grabbed his arm. 'Come, let us go home.'

She left George with the pictures of the 21 missing girls and asked him to keep on checking. The return trip to Aboke was even gloomier. Ben stared into the distance, rubbing his paralysed arm. Sister Rachele cried all the way back, for Monica, for Jenny, for all those thousands of forgotten children.

28

For I have redeemend them: And they shall increase as they have increased. And I will sow them among the people and they shall live with their children, and return again. (Zechariah 18, 8-9)

George was waiting impatiently at the gate of Gusco. The Sudanese visitors were expected any moment. He scanned the compound which had grown considerably in the past two years. Workshops for carpentry and general vocational training had been built. There were sewing classes for girls, as well as arithmetic and literacy courses to help the children regain some of the lost school years. Three enormous tents, donated by Unicef, had been erected at the far end of the compound, ready to receive hundreds of children at once.

It had never been, and would never be, like that November night in 1997. The army had been heavily criticised for parading the children through town. As a result, a child protection unit was set up at the military headquarters, manned by two nurses. George himself had played a part in the process of sensitising the soldiers and the community. Since then there had been few complaints about the army.

Fifteen hundred children had passed through his centre in the past two years. Some were only seven years old. Many thousands were still missing, including the Aboke girls. Since Sister Rachele had left him the list and the pictures, George had carefully kept track of the girls. He learnt that Angelina's daughter, Charlotte, had given birth to a baby boy in July 1998. It had been a difficult delivery – when she cried she was beaten – and she was taken to Juba hospital in a critical condition. But she survived and called her baby *Rubangakene*, Acholi for 'only God knows'. Another four Aboke girls had become mothers. Janet had given birth to a baby girl in December 1998 and called her child *Abed Kwene*: 'Where can I stay?' Two other girls had been given to commander Omona, who died of AIDS in a hospital in Khartoum at the end of 1997. Omona had had 52 wives. Nine of them had recently been released by the Lord's Resistance Movement. One arrived in May in a terminal stage of the disease and died three weeks later, a second one had herself tested but did not want to hear the result: she too was HIV-positive. 'We get our children back to bury them,' the parents had reacted bitterly.

George had also found confirmation of Jenny's death. A fifteen-year-old boy, who had recently returned, witnessed how she and another girl were beaten to death one morning in October 1997. They were later hung from a tree by their wrists. Their bodies were taken away in the night.

Four other Aboke girls were still with Kony. According to some accounts, Kony had now extended the number of his wives to sixty-seven. 'King Solomon also had between 600 and 800 wives and God never punished him,' he was reported a saying in one of his speeches. He preferred young girls, because they were free of AIDS. He promised to open a school for the hundreds of children who were already born in the camps in Sudan, and the Aboke girls were to be their teachers. But at other times he said the schoolgirls would be the ministers of his future government. The sister and the parents were 'annoying' him, he often complained. And he warned that even three lines of soldiers would not stop him: he would 'touch' the school of Aboke again.

George also learnt that Lagira, the commander who led the Aboke raid, had died on the battlefield in Sudan at the end of 1998. The news of Lagira's death had been received with general relief. The children who returned from his unit had often been the worst off. According to all witnesses, Lagira was one of the most cruel commanders of the Lord's Resistance Army.

But today the tents at Gusco were almost empty. It was George's biggest frustration. Not more than two dozen children had escaped all year. The rebels had not been much in the country either. The last attack dated from the end of January, when more than seventy children were abducted from one single village in Kitgum.

George didn't know how to explain this long period of quiet. Some said that the army had now firmly sealed off the border, preventing the rebels from entering. Others thought the Lord's Resistance Army had redirected their activities to Sudan. It was even reported that a battalion was sent to Congo to fight alongside Kabila's forces, against the rebels supported by Uganda. In a letter to the Organisation of African Unity, Kony had stated he would back Congolese President Kabila and escalate the war 'beyond diplomatic repair'. The British press even reported that Zimbabwe's President Mugabe, another of Kabila's allies, received Kony's representatives in his hotel room in London to sort out the deal. But George never met anybody who had actually been fighting in Congo.

For one thing, George knew the children were mainly involved in cultivating the land. According to the escapees, the Arabs were now only feeding those fighting the SPLA at the front line. The camps themselves were starving. At the end of the dry reason, up to ten children a day were reported to be dying of hunger and diarrhoea. Many others got killed or wounded on the battlefield in Sudan, not only by the SPLA but also by the Sudanese army. The escapees gave detailed accounts of these 'self-inflicted casualties': when a battle erupted, the Ugandan children stormed ahead, shooting while standing, while the Arabs threw themselves on the ground, crawling forwards and firing in front of them where they suspected the enemy to be, only to hit their own allies. Kony had reportedly been so disturbed about these casualties, that a new strategy was adopted: the Arab soldiers now surrounded an SPLA camp, Kony's rebels attacked, mostly in the early hours of the morning catching the enemy by surprise. As the Dinka fled, they ran straight into the arms of the Arabs. In this way, the returnees claimed, they were winning one battle after another.

From articles in the press, George concluded that the movement itself must be in serious disarray. Kony was constantly replacing his representatives abroad. The last spokesman in London, David Matsanga, stepped down in April 1999, claiming the LRA had become a 'Sudanese elite force, created to fight the SPLA and not Museveni.' He cited the Aboke girls as another reason for his resignation. 'The abduction, raping and kidnapping, especially of the Aboke girls, severely damaged the name of the LRA and put the movement in an indefensible position.' Only six months before, he had fiercely denied claims that Kony was operating from bases in Sudan.

But it was the fraud case that had tarnished their international reputation most. The new chairman of the Lord's Resistance Army, Powell Onen, was arrested in the UK in July 1998, not for his connection with the LRA but for defrauding the New Mexico City Council of US $4 million. The money was transferred to a bank account in Spain where the trail went cold. Onen was extradited to the US where, in a highly sensational case, he confessed his crimes. His properties, including a £340,000 mansion in fashionable Surrey and several expensive cars, were confiscated.

In order to restore the movement's image and collect new funds, the London branch had started an international public relations campaign. The mutilations of civilians, they claimed, were carried out by a special brigade of the Uganda government army, whose soldiers posed as rebels 'in order to tarnish the good name of the LRA'. They boasted a lot of financial support was coming from friends in Uganda and abroad. George knew this was true. While in London, one of his staff had been shown cheques, donated by ordinary British citizens.

The Gusco director would never forget the overseas message he received one day in July 1998. He had sent two children with a trauma counsellor to London to testify at a peace conference, organised by the large Acholi community in the UK. But all of a sudden, the children had disappeared. They were later found in the house of a representative of the Lord's Resistance Army, where they had been pressurised into signing a declaration withdrawing their testimonies. In return, the organisation would pay for their education in London. 'The children were brought here with fabricated stories to tarnish the good image of the Lord's Resistance Army. We tried to save the children from further indoctrination', the London branch had explained the incident.

George knew most of these 'representatives'. Some had been his schoolmates. They had once been rich and powerful people in the regimes of Obote and Okello. After Museveni's take-over, they fled to the UK where they were given political asylum. But they could not keep up their lavish lifestyles. Broke and desperate, they resorted to all means to return to power.

His thoughts were interrupted when a convoy of cars turned into the centre's gate. George got up to greet the visitors. They included the chairman and the deputy chairman of the Human Rights Committee of the Sudanese parliament. The delegation had come to assess the situation on the ground; to gather facts about the abductions by the Lord's Resistance Army and, eventually, to make arrangements for the repatriation of the children. The 'visit of the last hope', this latest Unicef initiative was dubbed. The Gusco director welcomed the visitors courteously and invited them into his office.

***

Sister Rachele entered George's office when the meeting was already under way. She took a seat at the back. Three years of searching for her girls had clearly taken their toll. Her hair had gone gray and her face showed deep marks of grief. Quietly, she listened to George's exposé. He was explaining the background to the conflict, the impact of the abductions on society and the centre's attempts to rehabilitate the children and bring reconciliation within the community.

George had been her lifeline with the girls in the past two years. Almost monthly she and the parents had visited Gusco to check for the latest news. And though it mostly had not been good news, they had somehow felt connected with the camps. She remembered the day Angelina heard about the birth of her grandchild. Being a midwife herself, the notion that she had not been there to assist her daughter at that critical moment had been a source of great pain. The woman had wondered whether she would ever be able to accept her grand child, fathered by a torturer and child rapist. Receiving the UN Prize for Peace at the end of 1998 had been of little consolation to Angelina. 'A prize for work not done,' she had told Kofi Annan bitterly, and he had answered: 'Consider it to be a sign of encouragement.'

While in New York, Angelina also had the chance to meet Olara Otunnu, the UN special representative for children and armed conflicts. Since he was a Ugandan and a former minister in the Okello regime, known personally by many LRA commanders, Angelina had hoped that he would help to get the girls released. But he simply told Angelina that the problem of child soldiers was a global issue and that he could not deal with the Ugandan case separately. In all those years, Otunnu had not once visited northern Uganda. And although the abducted children belonged to his own people, the Acholi, he never mentioned them in his interviews or speeches.

In spite of all that, Sister Rachele had never given up. The world had at last responded to their plea for help. In April 1998, the UN Commission for Human Rights had accepted a resolution demanding the immediate release of more than 10,000 abducted children. Sister Rachele had had an audience with Kofi Annan and with the pope, whom she thanked for his appeal. And Angelina had been received by Hilary Clinton in the White House. During the Clintons' visit to Uganda in March 1998, the American First Lady had strongly condemned the abduction of the Aboke girls and of thousands of other children.

'Perversely, the LRA claims to be doing the Lord's work, but there is no greater sin than forcing children to murder children, family members and even the parents who brought them into this world. There is no greater sin than raping young girls and sending them into slave labour. And there is no greater sin than using children as human shields in battle. The LRA call themselves soldiers, but they are cowards. For only cowards would hide behind children in battle.'

But these efforts did not secure the release of the girls. They had travelled half the world, they had seen the greatest of the earth, but the Aboke girls and thousands of other children remained in captivity. It had been Ben's greatest frustration. 'We have been in Sudan, South Africa, Europe and the United States to get our children released,' he used to lament. 'In vain.' His sudden death in April 1999 had been a serious blow to Sister Rachele and the Concerned Parents Association. Ever since they had received the news about Monica, he had not been the same. 'He died fighting for the Aboke girls,' the newspaper headline read. Thousands of mourners attended his funeral.

There had been one more attempt to secretly secure the release of the girls. In May 1998, Sister Rachele was contacted by the San Egidio Community in Rome, an Italian organisation involved in conflict resolution. She was told to leave for Gulu immediately. An aircraft would take her and a Red Cross representative to Orom, the place where the Aboke girls would be handed over. But it proved to be a trap: there was not even an airstrip in Orom.

'The release did not take place because Museveni sent 5000 heavily armed troops into the designated area,' Kony's spokesman later declared. 'They want to take me for a ride,' Museveni reacted angrily. 'These children will never be released unless we rescue them by force.' As a gesture of goodwill towards Sudan, he unilaterally freed some of the 114 Sudanese prisoners of war. The rest would follow, depending on Khartoum's help to release the 21 Aboke girls. But Kony rejected the linking of the two. He warned that any attempt to free the Aboke girls by force would result in their death.

George was finishing his exposé. The Sudanese MPs now turned to Sister Rachele, asking her particular questions about her visit to the camps in Sudan. She told them what she had witnessed: that Kony's camps were located next to Sudanese army camps, and that the last camp served as a buffer between the fighting parties in Sudan.

'Can we talk to some of the children?' the Sudanese finally asked.

George called about a dozen of them in. One boy described how he had been forced to kill a woman with a *panga*. A girl with a baby said she had been abducted at the age of 13, awarded to a commander as his wife and had given birth in the camp in Sudan. The children told their stories with visible difficulty, staring down, too ashamed to look up. It was too much for the Sudanese: they turned away and wept.

***

George looked at the children who were being questioned by the Sudanese visitors. They and many others had helped him to complete the puzzle, to penetrate into Kony's soul and answer the questions that had been on everybody's mind: What was the matter with this man? Why was he killing his own people?

The explanation was as logical as it was perverse. The Acholi people had become disloyal to him. They had turned away from him, like

Israel had turned away from God in the Old Testament. They had served foreign gods in their country: as teachers, civil servants or refugees, they had entered the government system and sided with the great enemy, Museveni. They ought to be punished for that. To Kony, he did not kill: he was 'cleansing' his people, so that only the pure ones would remain. And those pure ones were the children born in the camps in Sudan: a new and pure Acholi race that would one day become so numerous and powerful that it would overthrow the government of Uganda, and rule the country according to the Ten Commandments.

Epilogue

At the end of their visit in September 1999, the Sudanese MPs branded the atrocities of the Lord's Resistance Army as crimes against humanity. 'It is clear that the LRA are staying in Sudan with the knowledge and the consent of the Sudan government,' the chairman of the Human Rights Committee, Serag El Din Hamid Yousif, was quoted as saying in the local press. He announced that a Ugandan delegation would be invited to Sudan 'any time in September or October' to sort out the details of the repatriation. But an official invitation for a return visit never came.

In October 1999, the parliamentary assembly of the European Union and its partners of ACP (Africa, Caribbean and Pacific) almost unanimously condemned the abductions and atrocities of the Lord's Resistance Army during their meeting in Nassau, the Bahamas. The resolution called upon the government of Sudan to stop supporting Kony, to allow international organisations such as Unicef and the Red Cross access to the LRA camps, and to cooperate towards the immediate and unconditional release of all abducted children. The Sudanese delegation, which had hired a British lobbyist, distributed leaflets accusing the SPLA of forceful recruitment of children. In his intervention, the Sudanese spokesman claimed that the Lord's Resistance Army were operating outside areas controlled by the Sudanese government army.

A breakthrough came in December 1999. The Ugandan parliament passed the long-awaited Amnesty Bill, granting a full amnesty to all rebels who surrendered. The implementation of the Amnesty Act however, suffered serious delays. Kony himself rejected the offer of amnesty and said he intended to keep on fighting. In a recorded address, he lashed out at the Concerned Parents Association and vowed he would never release the Aboke girls.

On 8 December 1999, the presidents of Uganda and Sudan signed a historic agreement in Nairobi, mediated by the Carter Centre and President Moi. Both countries agreed to work towards restoring diplomatic relations. They also pledged to stop supporting each other's rebels and to return any abducted children. 'We will fully cooperate in the search and rescue of these victims, beginning immediately with those who can be identified,' the agreement read.

Kony apparently reacted furiously to the Nairobi Agreement. 'I lost so many soldiers because of Sudan and now Bashir turns his back on me,' he was quoted as saying. At the same time, Kony accused two of his top commanders of plotting to surrender with all the children, under the terms of the Amnesty Act. The commanders, Otti Lagony and Okello 'Director,' were detained and then sentenced to death by a military tribunal, chaired by Kony. They were reportedly killed by bayonets.

A force of 250 rebels invaded Uganda again just before Christmas 1999, after an absence of almost one year. One of their first acts of terror was the shelling of the house of the regional district commissioner in Gulu.

As the rebels continued killing, looting and abducting children throughout the year 2000, small numbers of abductees were repatriated as part of the Nairobi agreement. The first group of 21 Ugandans returned in January 2000. None, however, came directly from the camps. They had been taken by Unicef officials from hospitals or from houses in Juba where they were hiding. The second batch of 51 persons returned in April. Only eight of these appeared to be abducted children. Again nobody was taken from any of the LRA camps.

In July 2000, the European Parliament passed a resolution calling for the immediate implementation of the Nairobi agreement. It also called on international oil companies working in Sudan to halt their operations as long as abductions and slavery continued, and as long as there was no peaceful solution to the conflict in Sudan, following human rights reports that the oil was fuelling the war.

The government of Sudan was also criticised at the International Conference on War Affected Children in Winnipeg, Canada, in September 2000. This prompted both countries to sign another agreement: Sudan promised it would take all measures to ensure the release and safe return of more than six thousand abducted children, while the government of Uganda vowed to engage in dialogue with the LRA to persuade them to accept the offer of amnesty and reconciliation. As a result of the Winnipeg agreement, another eleven children were returned in October, including five young mothers with their babies.

A third initiative involved the foreign Ministers of Uganda, Sudan, Libya and Egypt. In August 2000, Sister Rachele visited Col. Gadaffi in Lybia. Both Libya and Egypt agreed to send monitors to the Sudan-Uganda border to verify any arms trafficking. Together with Unicef and the Carter Centre a detailed timeframe was worked out for the relocation, disarmement and disbandment of the LRA. All abducted children would be repatriated by the end of 2000, starting with the Aboke girls on October 15th. It was considered the most important break-through since the signing of the Nairobi agreement.

In October 2000, Sister Rachele and Angelina spent two weeks in Khartoum, waiting for the green light to go to Juba and identify the Aboke girls. However, nothing happened and they returned to Uganda empty-handed. It seemed the LRA leadership had not yet agreed to any of the proposals. A press release by the Carter Centre at the end of November stated that a meeting was to take place soon between Joseph Kony and a delegation of senior government officials, Acholi leaders and representatives of the Carter Centre and Unicef. But Kony failed to turn up at the set date in January 2001. The deployment of the observer team at the Uganda-Sudan border was hindered by the outbreak of an ebola epidemic in northern Uganda.

By March 2001, twenty Aboke girls were still missing. The last girl returned in April 2000. She had escaped from the Nisitu camp in July 1999 and had been hidden by a charcoal man in Juba for five months. He reportedly forced her to be his wife in exchange for protection. She managed to run away from him and was taken to Torit with two other escaped boys by a commander of the Equatorial Defence Forces, another local militia fighting alongside the Sudanese armed forces. But instead of releasing them, the boys were taken to the battlefield, while the Aboke girl was kept by one of the commanders. She fell seriously ill. A medical test disclosed she was pregnant. After two months, the three were eventually released and marched to Uganda by Sudanese escorts. On the way, in the mountains, the girl had a miscarriage. One of the boys took care of her. They finally crossed the Ugandan border on April 20.

In the year 2000, more than four hundred children were again abducted by rebels of the Lord's Resistance Army; one was only two years old...